Opting for Change

A Handbook on Evaluation and Planning for Theological Education by Extension

F. Ross Kinsler and James H. Emery
Editors

William Carey Library
Pasadena, California

Programme on Theological Education
World Council of Churches
Geneva, Switzerland

SPECIAL NOTE

This manual has been produced in a special page perforation, 3-hole binding which makes it possible to remove text, worksheets and exercises adn reproduce them for classroom use without first having to obtain permission from the publisher. (See page vi in Introduction.)

Co-Published by
WILLIAM CAREY LIBRARY
P.O. Box 40129
Pasadena, California 91114 U.S.A.
ISBN 0-87808-229-8
and
WORLD COUNCIL OF CHURCHES
Programme on Theological Education
150 route de Ferney
1211 Geneva 20, Switzerland
ISBN 2-8254-1026-8

Library of Congress #91-65731

Illustrations on the cover and in the text are from *WHERE THERE IS LIFE AND STRUGGLE, The Art of Rini Tempelton*, published by Real Comet Press, Seattle, Washington, and used by permission.

PRINTED IN THE UNITED STATES OF AMERICA

Contents

Contributors

Dale Bisnauth is a former director of the Guyana Extension Seminary. He currently serves on the staff of the Caribbean Council of Churches (P.O. Box 616, Bridgetown, Barbados).

Fernando Cascante, a young Costa Rican pastor and teacher, is finishing graduate studies in the U.S.A. with a dissertation on "Curriculum and Ecclesiology in TEE: A Study of their Relationship in Two Programs." (Apartado 901—1000, San Jose, Costa Rica)

James Emery, currently on the staff at Missionary Internship near Detroit, played a major role in the design and development of the pioneer TEE program in Guatemala. (P.O. Box 457, Farmington, Michigan 48332, U.S.A.)

David Esterline has served as a theological teacher in Cameroun and Fiji. His dissertation at the Graduate Theological Union, Berkeley was entitled "A Proposal for the Evaluation of Theological Education by Extension." (Pacific Theological College, P.O. Box 388, Suva, Fiji)

Patricia Harrison has for many years been a consultant and trainer for TEE, particulalrly in the Pacific, Asia, and Australia-New Zealand. (11 Garibaldi Street, Armidale NSW 2350, Australia)

Ross Kinsler, currently on the staff of the Latin American Biblical Seminary in Costa Rica, was involved in the development of TEE in Guatemala and later served on the staff of the Program on Theological Education of the WCC. (Apartado 901—1000, San Jose, Costa Rica)

Samuel Satyaranjan has for many years been Registrar for the Senate of Serampore College, which sets examinations and grants degrees for some 35 theological institutions throughout India. (Senate of Serampore College, Serampore 712201, Hooghly District, West Bengal, India)

Introduction

Parallel to developments in other fields of human development, theological education by extension has been a quiet, growing movement for renewal and change in many parts of the world. The World Council of Churches' Program on Theological Education, having accompanied and supported this movement for many years, sponsored a consultation on evaluation of TEE programs in Costa Rica in May, 1990. Representatives of extension programs from most regions of the world gathered to share their experiences and concerns, to consider evaluation models and issues, and to recommend further evaluation efforts. They proposed the elaboration of a handbook for evaluation of TEE programs, which has led to this publication. This handbook is a first fruit of the Costa Rica consultation and more specifically of a small working group that met subsequently in Serampore, India: Dale Bisnauth (Guyana), Patricia Harrison (Australia), Fernando Cascante (Costa Rica), Samuel Satyaranjan (India), and Ross Kinsler (Costa Rica). David Esterline (Fiji), provided additional major input. Final writing and editing fell to Ross Kinsler and James Emery (U.S.A.).

What is TEE?

Theological education by extension has been defined in many different ways; it has taken many different forms; and it is being used in many different ways for many different purposes in many different contexts. Common and distinctive to all TEE programs is the combination of three basic program components: ongoing guided study, ongoing practice of ministry, and regular seminar meetings to integrate and reinforce study and practice. Students normally maintain their family, employment, and local church and community roots, which has enormous theological, educational, sociological, and economic implications, in contrast to residential or full-time programs that take their students out of the normal mainstream of their lives. Extension students receive regular, frequent guidance and motivation through seminar meetings with peers and itinerant professors or adjunct facilitators, which is very different from the isolation of correspondence and other distance programs. TEE programs should be considered formal theological education if they offer academic and/or ministerial credentials, as do more traditional, centralized programs; they should be considered non-formal if they do not. The quality of each extension program should be evaluated, just as every residential program should be evaluated, on the basis of contextual realities and stated goals. The recognition of extension studies may depend not only on the quality of the program but also on dominant views of education in the local context; these may change as more schools and universities establish alternative, decentralized patterns of formal education.

What are the Purposes of Evaluation?

Theological institutions have traditionally assessed their students' academic achievement through examinations and other written assignments. In some countries the theological institutions have formed associations in order to provide accreditation standards and procedures by which potential students, their churches, and the public can have some idea of the levels of their programs, resources, and degrees. This handbook is concerned primarily about self-evaluation in relation to planning, i. e. about ways in which people who are engaged in TEE can clarify their goals, review all aspects of their programs in relation to those goals, and assess results in order to pursue their goals more effectively.

TEE is often portrayed as a vision and a movement for the renewal of ministry in the church and in the world. The task of evaluation is to translate that vision into concepts and criteria that can be applied to the various components of the respective TEE programs. More specifically the task of evaluation is to articulate the educational design and identify guidelines for the essential learning resources, experiences, and procedures that make up each TEE program. Informal evaluation takes place quite naturally whenever students discuss their learning experiences, whenever faculties plan and review their work, whenever administrators work out their budgets and reports, and whenever congregations, pastors, and church bodies criticize or commend the graduates of these programs. This handbook provides resources for more careful, more systematic, more scientific ways to enable these and other interested parties to make critical evaluations and contribute to the ongoing planning processes of our TEE programs.

How to Use This Handbook

Perhaps few will want to read through this handbook from beginning to end. It is, after all, a handbook. Depending on local needs and interest, we recommend that readers take these steps:

1. Look through the table of contents in order to see what articles and tools are included.

2. Read those articles and/or tools that will be most useful for reflection with your colleagues and friends.

3. Reflect on the history and needs of your program as you consider exercises for your use with colleagues and friends.

4. Copy and distribute materials that you consider pertinent—first to a few colleagues to stimulate their interest and get their comments.

5. Note that these materials are only suggestive; they should be adapted for each context and program; you may well want to add your own ideas, make changes and develop additional materials.

6. Work out with your faculty, student body, board of directors, church leaders, etc. plans for specific and comprehensive, immediate and longterm evaluations.

7. Make evaluation and planning an integral part of your work, an essential vehicle for improvement and progress.

PART I contains the only lengthy articles in the handbook. Each essay contains important material for discussion about evaluation of theological education by extension or, for that matter, about theological education in general. The third article ends with a complete sample evaluation workbook.

PART II is called "Tools for Reflection on Basic Issues in Theological Education." It contains 16 exercises that are self-contained but can be put together in any combination for workshops, consultations, and seminars or colloquias among theological educators, students, and church leaders as they consider the challenges and short-comings, problems and possibilities of theological education in diverse situations around the world. These tools have been grouped together, somewhat arbitrarily, under these topics: "Theological and Educational Foundations," "Spiritual Formation," "Structures, Ideology, and Values," and "Contextualization and Globalization"—major issues for all kinds of theological education, not just TEE.

PART III is more specifically directed to "Tools for Evaluation and Planning of TEE Programs." It offers another 16 exercises dealing with "Curriculum," "Study Materials, Experiential Learning, and Seminars," "Students," and "Facilitators," i.e., the basic ingredients of TEE programs.

These materials have been put together by people from different parts of the world, different church traditions and cultural backgrounds, and different theological and ideological perspectives. There has been no attempt to harmonize their styles or their viewpoints. Users of the handbook are encouraged to make their own adjustments, adaptations, and additions to these materials so that they will indeed be effective tools for evaluation and planning of theological education in their particular contexts.

During the last 25 years TEE has challenged many of the assumptions and myths about theological education. It has demonstrated that significant and unimagined changes are possible in the way we do theological education. The fervent desire of all who have participated in this project is that more careful evaluation and planning will not only consolidate and improve the changes of recent years, but challenge us all to more critical reflection, more creative innovation, and above all more faithful obedience to the One who gave his life that all might have life as God intended.

The entire Handbook is designed with perforated pages and three holes so that users will tear out articles and exercises that interest them, photocopy and distribute them among colleagues (teachers, students, administrators, boards, graduates, church ministry committees, pastors, etc.) for evaluation and planning meetings and workshops, and then keep the originals for future use.

Part I: The Challenge

- Theological Education by Extension:
  A Vision and a Challenge

- A Survey of Approaches to Evaluation

- Community-Based Evaluation

- Accreditation and Theological Education

Theological Education by Extension: A Vision and a Movement

When a small group of theological educators launched their extension plan in Guatemala in 1963, they were responding to very concrete leadership needs in their local, multi-cultural, and deeply impoverished context. But they, and soon many others, realized that simple, basic changes in the way we do theological education could open up our vision of the church and its ministry, create new and significant possibilities for mission, and profoundly re-shape our understanding of theological education itself. As more and more people, institutions, and churches entered this process, they created a movement for ongoing change, gathering and incorporating insights and resources from diverse church traditions, cultural contexts, and socio-educational fields.

The following reflections are intended to enumerate some of these insights and resources in order to encourage those who are engaged in this movement to continue deepening and expanding the vision and others to join the movement and add their insights and resources. These lessons from the last 28 years should challenge us to greater creativity as we face urgent, greatly enlarged leadership needs in the years to come.

As with other movements, the force of theological education by extension is to be found in the correlation between form and substance, between the new structures-methods-materials and new understandings and goals, between movement and vision. The inspiration and the challenge to change have come from those who had previously been excluded from formal patterns of theological education and have thus been excluded from formally recognized ministry. As the following outline suggests, TEE has been and continues to be a movement for the full incorporation of God's people in ministry, mission, and theology.

Ministry by the People
- **Overcoming academic, clerical, and professional limitations**
- **Overcoming limitations of class, gender, race, culture, and age**
- **Overcoming dependence and elitism**

Mission by the People
- **Contextualizing the Gospel, the church, and its mission and ministry**
- Awakening God's people for their mission
- Engaging God's people in their theological vocation.

Theology by the People
- **Seeing the world from the underside**
- **Rereading the Bible and rearticulating the faith**
- **Recreating the church, its ministry, and mission**

TEE: A Vehicle for Ongoing Personal, Ecclesial, and Social Transformation

For personal reflection and group discussion:
1. *What has been my/our contact or experience with TEE?*
2. *How would I/we describe the vision of this movement?*

MINISTRY BY THE PEOPLE

Overcoming Academic, Clerical, and Professional Limitations

A favorite text of the extension movement has been Ephesians 4:11-16, and all who are concerned about theological education are well advised to keep this dynamic teaching before them. Whatever the institutional forms of the church's ministry, it must respond to these clear guidelines:

- Christ has given to the church many ministries, not just one, and they are distributed among many members, not concentrated in one office.
- These ministers/servants are called to equip all the saints/members for the work of ministry, not primarily to do that work themselves, certainly not to monopolize it.
- The work of ministry is all that extends and builds up the body of Christ, not just and not particularly those sacramental, liturgical, preaching, and governance tasks traditionally identified with the ordained ministry.
- The body of believers is to be built up to maturity in order to minister to others. Thus the ministries within the context of the church are to edify it both in numbers and maturity, in order to serve and call the whole of creation to Christ.

3

- The failure to incorporate all the members in this work of mutual ministry and in service and witness to the world is what causes so many to be carried about by new doctrines and controversies.
- Growth in Christ's body requires, as the text repeats again and again, the participation of every member.

Surely theological education should be guided by these clear principles of the nature of the church's ministry.

While different forms of theological education have developed down through the twenty centuries of church history, the dominant current models developed in North America and Europe in the 1800's and have since then been exported throughout the world through the missionary movement. With notable exceptions these models have, whatever their stated goals, tended strongly to the elevation of a highly trained, ordained, professional class of ministers at the expense of the participation of the whole body of Christ. This elitist tendency has been increasingly reinforced by societies, both north and south, progressively committed to academically and professionally credentialed specialists in every field. Ironically, training for the ministry was the first to specialize and require superior and separate schools in North America; now theological schools everywhere are pressed to create and maintain requirements more or less equivalent to the other professions, though they only became viable in the U. S. after World War II and are still not viable for large sectors of the U. S. churches even today.

Theological education by extension was born out of the contradiction between the dynamic, biblical model of ministry and the elitist North Atlantic model. Transferred to Third World contexts where only 1-5% of the population qualifies for any form of university training, that model proved to be totally inadequate. TEE experiments all over Latin America, Africa and Asia, and also parts of North America and Europe have demonstrated that theological education can be made accessible to the whole church throughout large geographical areas, multi-cultural societies, and diverse educational levels. To the surprise of some these new models have reached persons of "higher" as well as "lower" academic and socio-economic levels, and they have opened the doors of ministry to a wide spectrum of the church's leadership, whether they are candidates for ordination or not.

For personal reflection and group discussion:

1. *To what extent have the traditional theological institutions in my/our country/church fulfilled or denied the Ephesians 4:11-16 understandings of ministry and who should carry it on?*

2. *To what extent have the new extension programs fulfilled or denied the Ephesians 4:11-16 understandings of ministry?*

3. *To what extent have all of the ministries been activated, the apostolate, evangelists, and prophets reaching out to the whole community as well as the pastor-teachers within the congregations?*

Overcoming Limitations of Class, Gender, Race, Culture, and Age

The New Testament presents an understanding of the church that is all-inclusive. The Gospels describe Jesus' option for the poor, women, "publicans and sinners," children, and even foreigners, while he expended much of this time and energy on the scribes and Pharisees and other representatives of the power structures. Although Paul's writings reflect unquestioned social and economic and cultural patterns, he summarized the inclusive nature of the church in Galatians 3:28; "There is neither Jew nor Greek, there is neither slave nor free, there is neither male nor female; for you are all one in Christ Jesus." Surely theological education should be a critical vehicle for building and expressing an inclusive ministry for an inclusive church.

The record of formal theological education has been, until quite recently, very exclusive, whatever its good intentions. A major problem has been the logic and economics of the ordained ministry. It has seemed reasonable and necessary to offer theological education for those who where en route to becoming pastors; limited funds should be invested in those who would spend their lives in "fulltime ministry." Thus those who did not meet the requirements of ordained ministry have been excluded: the poor, lesser educated, women, racial and ethnic minorities, and older persons with family and employment commitments. In recent years some high level seminaries have sought to recruit minority leaders, but there are serious questions about the relevance of the orientation they receive and expectations that their training provokes. In those countries and churches where women are now given access to ordained ministry their enrollment in the seminaries has jumped dramatically and their potential impact on the church's ministry is considerable, but the framework is still professional, ordained ministry.

Theological education by extension offers a radically different panorama with regard to the traditional limitations of class, gender, ethnic group, race, culture, and age. The logic and economics of ordained ministry break down, and all sectors of the church can readily be given access. Some extension programs have of course been directed toward candidates for ordained ministry or lay leaders or experienced clergy, but any network of extension can open its doors to include others at little or no additional expense. In many cases women are studying theology even though they are not yet admitted to ordained ministry. Likewise lay persons not seeking ordination and persons of diverse academic levels are actually laying the foundation for a more inclusive ministry. Racial and ethnic minorities are much more likely to take advantage of and enjoy the fruits of decentralized and contextualized theological education, as are older persons in general.

> For personal reflection and group discussion:
>
> 1. *How effective have our traditional theological institutions been with regard to the training and incorporation of poor, less schooled, women, racial and ethnic minorities, and older candidates for lay and ordained ministries in church and society?*
>
> 2. *How effective have the new extension programs been in this regard? Are they simply preparing people for traditional and institutional ministries?*
>
> 3. *Has the vision of extending the mission and ministries been opened up to create new possibilities of service and witness?*

Overcoming Dependence and Elitism

The reign of God, which Jesus announced and lived and we are called to announce and live, comes not through the rich and powerful and highly educated; it emerges among the poor and despised and powerless. If the church is to serve God's reign, it must somehow select and train leaders who represent and treasure and communicate the perspectives and values of the oppressed and marginalized. How then should theological education be structured? Where should it be located? What kind of a curriculum is required?

As we have noted above, theological education has largely adopted the forms and levels and styles and assumptions of higher education, which is large-

ly a negation of the values and style of God's reign. The basic assumption has been that the benefits of such education will "trickle down" to the "lower" levels of the church, to the laity, to minorities, to women, to the poor. Efforts are periodically made to provide theological students with inner city or minority or Third World experience in order to broaden or challenge or complement their privileged and isolated institutional reality, but such experiences are only the exception that proves the rule of elitist education for a dependent church.

Once again TEE offers a significantly alternative approach. Extension students not only represent the whole spectrum of church and society; their training takes place in those diverse contexts. Granted that the curriculum, methods, and theological perspectives are determined largely by those who run the programs, the potential for genuinely contextual education rooted in the realities of an unjust and sinful world and the perspectives of the poor and excluded is given. Unfortunately extension programs often find themselves pressed to meet the "standards" and expectations of centralized institutions and their accrediting associations and make little use of their greatest resource, the context and experiences of their students.

> For personal reflection and group discussion.
>
> 1. *How well do current (traditional or extension) theological education programs in my/our country/church represent and treasure and communicate the perspectives and values of oppressed and marginalized people?*
>
> 2. *How could the majority of people who are poor and without power or extensive resources become full participants?*

MISSION BY THE PEOPLE

Promoting Contextualization of the Gospel, the Church, and its Mission and Ministry

The current focus on contextualization was launched some 20 years ago; its theological foundation is the incarnation. The challenge of contextualization is particularly important for theological education, because of the latter's role in the formation and training of those who carry responsibility for leading the church in proclaiming and living the Gospel. Earlier discussions about indigenization were concerned with the cultural and religious forms that the Gospel, the church, and its ministry should adopt in order to be authentic expressions of God's incarnate love in every context. The contextualization debate has gone on to consider the social and economic structures that express or deny the incarnation of God's justice and peace. It has become increasingly clear that Jesus called his followers not only to demonstrate God's love within the cultural and religious forms of every time and place but also to resist and transform the social and economic structures that oppress and diminish and destroy life. The church and its ministry should be genuine expressions of God's love, justice, and peace in each cultural context.

Theological education has naturally reflected or imitated the dominant educational patterns in each country, whether those patterns are indigenous or imported. It tends to pass on, consciously or unconsciously, intentionally or unintentionally, the assumptions and values of the dominant culture. Thus young (male) candidates for the ordained ministry have for decades gone off to the capital cities or to convents for special training in a special environment. Though they are apparently responding to a call to special sacrifice, they are actually preparing for special privilege and power in the church. In this process they are uprooted and distanced from their various socio-economic and cultural contexts.

Theological education by extension is an attempt to reverse this process of decontextualization, of alienation, to give the local church's natural leadership access to theological education in their own cultural contexts, and to enable those local leaders to shape their own ministry, the churches' life, and its evangelistic and social witness according to their reading of the Bible and of their world. As God's people deepen their understanding of their mission and ministry, they will be challenged to create new forms of service and extend God's Reign to the ends of the earth.

As many have pointed out, the extension education network can be an efficient instrument of theological and cultural imperialism, imposing fixed formulas and contents and values. But it can also be an effective instrument for the incarnation/ contextualizaton of the Gospel of God's reign in the local community in accord with their life and customs.

For personal reflection and group discussion:

1. *In what ways do current theological education programs reflect dominant educational patterns and pass on the assumptions and values of the dominant culture?*

2. *In what ways do current theological education programs enable the church and its ministry to challenge dominant cultural values and social structures that deny God's justice and peace.*

Awakening God's People for their Mission

Incarnation-contextualization is a fundamental guideline for the structures of theological education, which determine who has access, who sets the agenda, who provides the context. Conscientization, or encouraging people to understand their own world and situation, is a critical guideline for the methodology of theological education, i.e. the educational or learning process. If we understand the church to be an organic body in which all are subjects, ministering to each other in myriad ways, and extend God's Reign to all peoples, then theological education should work in the same way. Paulo Freire presents an educational philosophy and methodology in which adult learners, even at the most basic level of literacy, are not receptacles to be filled or animals to be trained but persons to be awakened to their human potential through dialogue with other human beings about the real world. Traditional schooling has largely been a process of domestication, in which the participants, whether adults or children, are led passively or forcibly, by rewards and punishments, through programs designed and imposed by others.

Traditional theological education has also, with varying degrees of sophistication and erudition, treated its students, at least to some degree, as objects to be led through a long series of courses, assignments, and examinations developed by those who know for those who are ignorant. For extremely dogmatic traditions this kind of indoctrination may be very acceptable; for those traditions that affirm God's presence among all God's people it is unacceptable. Somehow the students must become the subjects of theological learning in community with living and recorded representatives of the wider church and society, past and present.

By incorporating not just young candidates for ministry but all sectors of the church, particularly its natural leaders in every social and cultural context, TEE has had the possibility of changing the traditional educational patterns and becoming a genuine process of conscientization in community. If mature students bring to the learning process their experience of life and ministry, if their program provides a serious encounter with the life and ministry of God's people throughout the Bible, down through history, and around the world, then genuine theological learning and ministerial formation can take place.

More than 95 percent of the churches' resources are used to maintain and enhance the existing faith communities. Theological education must also extend people's vision for the evangelization of the whole world. If our God is in fact the God of all creation, surely this aspect of God's covenant and promise must challenge the churches.

For personal reflection and group discussion:

1. *To what extent and in what ways do existing programs of theological education lead their students through an established process of domestication.*

2. *To what extent and in what ways do existing programs awaken all God's people for ministry and mission?*

Engaging People in their Theological Vocation

Third World theologians, women, First World minorities, and representatives of poor and marginalized people everywhere have in recent years demonstrated clearly and powerfully that the Gospel of God's reign is a message of liberation, beginning with the Exodus, which is the Old Testament paradigm of salvation, and with Jesus, who declared from the outset that his ministry was/is "to preach good news to the poor . . . to proclaim release to the captives and recovering of sight to the blind, to set at liberty those who are oppressed, to proclaim the acceptable (Jubilee) year of the Lord." The contemporary voices mentioned at the beginning of this paragraph have also claimed rightfully that theology itself must be freed from its North Atlantic cultural, philosophical, and ideological captivity so that these new voices from the underside can be heard.

Traditional theological institutions have of course given priority to the intellectual giants of theology, who have largely lived and reflected, spoken and written within and from the upper echelons of the socio-economic-educational strata of church and society. These institutions themselves—their curricula and personnel and lifestyle—have largely emulated the university model, insofar as their economic resources permit. Today, theological education requires another base that will be capable of penetrating the frontiers of class, gender, race, culture, and age.

Theological education by extension has attempted to provide that new base by bringing together local leaders in their own contexts and developing with them essential biblical, theological, and pastoral tools and perspectives for their ministerial and theological vocation. The challenge is not to bring these local leaders "up to" our academic standards so much as it is to adapt our academic resources to their realities and experiences. The difficulty is not so much to get them to understand the resources we can offer so much as it is to understand the resources they can provide. TEE has barely begun the process of freeing theology and creating theologies that speak to the problems and needs of people where they are.

For personal reflection and group discussion:

1. *How are the theological education programs in my/our church/country contributing to the process of freeing theology from its traditional limitations and making it responsive to the needs of people around the world?*

2. *What should these programs do in the future to stimulate and equip people to think through their own situations in terms of biblical perspectives and vision?*

THEOLOGY BY THE PEOPLE

Seeing the World from the Underside

Latin American, Asian, African, feminist, and other contemporary theologians share basic perspectives on what is referred to as "the hermeneutical circle," which might also be called "the pedagogical circle." Whatever else it does, theological education must today respond to their challenge to:

- **see the world from the underside, where most people in the world live, as did the biblical writers**
- **reread the Bible, theology, the faith from that perspective, and**
- **recreate the church, its ministry, and mission.**

This permanent process implies an epistemological breakthrough, as previous, uncritical and unhistorical, often pietistic and idealistic, fundamentalist or liberal perspectives are dramatically challenged by the view of the world and the faith and the church's ministry from the underside.

In many Third World countries theological institutions are still in the process of equipping and incorporating national faculty members, usually men who obtain their advanced degrees in First World

7

institutions and join the intellectual elites of their own societies. In First World countries theological institutions are attempting to incorporate women and minority professors, but the dominant view is still from the top, so these new theological voices often feel that they are being exploited, domesticated, or coopted.

TEE offers the possibility of building its entire learning process on the view of the world from the perspective of the poor and marginalized, because its primary context is the real world—local communities and congregations and cultures and peoples—rather than artificial classroom settings. Certainly faculties must be representative of those excluded from resources and power; critical tools for social analysis must be provided; course work and materials must open up the macro and micro-reality of the local contexts. But the epistemological breakthrough requires an existential encounter with the structures and the pain of injustice as only the oppressed know them.

> For personal reflection and group discussion:
>
> 1. *Do current theological education programs enable their students and churches to see the world from the underside?*
>
> 2. *How could they do so more effectively in the future?*

Rereading the Bible and Rearticulating the Faith

The second fundamental element in the engagement of God's people in their theological vocation is to reread or rediscover the biblical faith in light of the new understandings of reality from the underside. For many the Bible has come alive powerfully when they realize that it was written by and for oppressed people, that its message is not so much concerned about proving the existence of God as it is about declaring God's presence with and for the poor, the suffering and those rejected by society, that the history of salvation is a movement of healing, wholeness, justice, and peace for all people. Key texts—such as the Jubilee passages in Leviticus, Deuteronomy, Isaiah, and Luke—illuminate dramatically not only the biblical message but the central historical problems (the land, debts, slavery) of our own time and our own world. Even somewhat discarded books of the Pentateuch, the Wisdom Literature, and the Apocalypse of Daniel and Revelation become surprisingly meaningful as expressions of God's people's struggle to be faithful in the face of external and internal corruption, oppression, and imperialism.

Theological schools have generally been concerned with the task of passing on the biblical faith from within major historical and theological traditions. They have attempted to equip their students with critical tools with which they can examine for themselves the strengths and weaknesses of these traditions. But relatively little has been done to reread the Bible and rearticulate the faith and contextualize theology out of the living testimony of God's people here and now.

TEE is peculiarly suited for this task, which may be considered to be primary. Certainly all extension students will need to confront the major historical and theological traditions of the past and of the world church today. But these studies themselves will take on new vitality if they are linked directly to the challenge of incarnating and articulating the faith in and for each local context. These theological students will then realize that they stand not at the periphery but at the forefront of the theological enterprise.

> For personal reflection and group discussion:
>
> 1. *Are current theological education programs enabling their students and churches to reread the Bible and rearticulate the faith out of the living testimony of God's people here and now?*
>
> 2. *How could they do so more effectively in the future?*

Recreating the Church, Its Ministry, and Mission

Finally, Third World, feminist, African, and other contemporary theologians challenge us all to recreate the church, its ministry, and mission from the perspective of the faith as seen from the underside of history. The base ecclesial communities of Latin America have coined the term "ecclesiogenesis." Feminists in North America speak of "woman church." Others have used ancient and contemporary myths, religions, personalities , and art to recover the indigenous faces of the God who has so long been Europeanized and thus diminished for all of us, but particularly for those peoples who retain cultural and affective and communal dimensions of life largely lost to the First World.

One has only to witness an Orthodox liturgy in North Sudan or South India, the Peasant Mass in Nicaragua, Black hymnody in downtown Los Angeles or the Southside of Chicago, the worship of large and small spiritual churches throughout Africa to know that theology and theological education as established by the Western missionary movement and dominated by academic institutional models are not adequate for responding to present and future needs of the churches. Rather, theology and theological education will have to go back to their roots in the living faith of God's people, which is bursting out with enormous vitality even in the midst of unprecedented suffering and sacrifice.

Theological education by extension offers an enormous, flexible framework for this task. First there must be a new, far more dynamic vision which will seek not simply to repeat or extend but to recreate the church, its ministry, and mission. Then there will have to be valiant and vigorous attempts to evaluate and redirect programs, curricula, and resources to carry out that vision. Finally there needs to be a very large dose of humility in order to recognize where God is acting and learn from those who are experiencing God's presence in our contemporary history.

For personal reflection and group discussion:

1. *In what ways are current theological education programs rooted in the living faith of God's people and recreating the church, its ministry and mission?*

2. *How could they do this more effectively in the future?*

TEE: A VEHICLE FOR ONGOING PERSONAL, ECCLESIAL, AND SOCIAL TRANSFORMATION

Throughout this paper we have referred constantly to the nature of ministry, the nature of the church, and the nature of God's reign. If God rules as sovereign over all life, overcoming false dualisms between the spiritual and the material, piety and politics, soul and body, then the church and its ministry must work toward the redemption and integration of all of life in God's peace (shalom). That peace can only be achieved through love and justice, which requires personal, ecclesial, and social transformation (conversion). The universal propensity to selfishness, exploitation, oppression, and violence is a denial of our humanity and a call to an ever more comprehensive evangelization, a far more profound spirituality, a more realistic and historic theology.

Theological education is not the only key to unlock the doors to change, conversion, transformation. It has often been the key that locks those doors. But the TEE movement has years gathered clues and perspectives and experiences that offer new possibilities that can open those doors.

A vision and a movement. The vision affirms that God's reign is breaking in, as in Jesus' ministry, among the poor, the outcast, and the marginalized, offering hope for new life in faith, new faith communities, new expressions of a just and peaceful society. The extension movement is being challenged and challenging the church to grasp the opportunity to form radical disciples, to build faithful communities, to reread the Bible and do theology, to enter fully into God's historic, saving mission in every place in response to every human need and to the whole creation.

For personal reflection and group discussion:

1. *What priorities should the churches put before the TEE movement under the vision of God's reign on earth as in heaven?*

2. *What priorities should the TEE movement put before the churches?*

A Survey of Approaches to Evaluation

Over the past 20 years there has been an outpouring of publications relating to educational program evaluation; several completely new models have been introduced, variations on established approaches have been presented, and discussions continue on every aspect of theory and practice.[1] A review of the primary definitions of evaluation and an outline of some of the more prominent program evaluation models may be helpful as background for the discussion of the evaluation of TEE.

Possibly the best known definition of evaluation is that contained in the objectives approach of Ralph W. Tyler, the man usually referred to as the father of educational evaluation and whose influence is still widely felt. Tyler understood educational curriculum as a design to help students achieve specific behavioral objectives and "education evaluation" (a phrase which he coined) as the assessment of the extent to which those objectives were achieved in an educational program. His primary point was that specified objectives should provide the basis for all related decisions, for planning, selection of materials, development of procedures, and, from the evaluation perspective, these objectives should provide the criteria by which the students' achievements should be measured. Thus, in objectives based studies, the advance organizers[2] are the program's stated objectives, and the purpose is to establish the extent to which the objectives are being met.

> The process of evaluation is essentially the process of determining to what extent the educational objectives are actually being realized. . . Since educational objectives are essentially changes in human beings, that is, the objectives aimed at are to produce certain desirable changes in the behavior patterns of the students, then evaluation is the process for determining the degree to which these changes in behavior are actually taking place.[3]

The appeal of Tyler's approach is quite easy to understand; it was simple to grasp, it possessed an internal logic, and it constituted a great advance over the prevailing emphasis on measurement. Before Tyler's time evaluation was understood primarily as the measurement of pupil achievement, with the judgment of individual students in relation to established norms receiving the most attention. Tyler made it clear that such measurement was only one of the many tools to be used in evaluation and that evaluation should be thought of in very broad terms.

Another reason for the success of Tyler's model is that it provided a scientific approach with its pre/post formula. Behavior was to be measured twice, before and after "treatment," a plan that fit very nicely with the experimental designs being used by other behavioral sciences, and one which followed the usual and time-honored methods of the physical sciences.[4] In the field of adult education, as in education in general, Tyler remains extremely influential.

When the Russians launched Sputnik in 1957, the U.S. government reacted by pouring millions of dollars into new education programs, programs which eventually needed to be evaluated.[5] Before long, however, the educators involved in the new programs complained that the evaluation efforts were not offering any real service. In 1963 Lee Cronback responded with "Course Improvement through Evaluation," criticizing evaluations for their lack of usefulness and relevance and calling for attention to the needs of decision makers. His primary point was that education planners would be much better served if evaluation would focus on the decisions that have to be made while the program is being developed rather than concentrating on whether certain objectives are being achieved. He defined evaluation as "the collection and use of information to make decisions about an educational program."[6] In short, he recommended that the primary organizer for evaluation be shifted from objectives to the information needs of decision makers. Who are the decision makers? What decisions need to be made? What are the values on which the decisions will be based? He emphasized that greater benefit will result if a course can be improved while it is still "fluid" than if the evaluation knowledge does not become available until the product is on the market.

Other papers followed, pointing out the problems with contemporary evaluation practice and suggesting new models. In Michael Scriven's 1967 essay,[7] the now well-known distinction between formative (improving) and summative (judging) evaluation was introduced. Formative evaluation has to do with the formation and planning of a proposed program and the development and improvement of an on-going one, while summative has to do with the establishment of accountability, final worth, or accreditation. Scriven also argued for the centrality of values in evaluation; he goes beyond the question of establishing the relationship between objectives and achievement and affirms that the program under evaluation cannot be considered valuable unless the objectives that have been achieved are themselves worthwhile.[8] This is echoed in the adult education field with the indication that education takes place only when what is taught and learned has value.[9]

The understanding that judgment lies at or near the center of evaluation can be found in many definitions. Daniel Stufflebeam's 1975 statement provides an example: "Evaluation is the act of examining and judging, concerning the worth, quality, significance, amount, degree or condition of something. In short, evaluation is the ascertainment of merit." The definition in the *Standards for Evaluation of Educational Programs, Projects, and Materials* of 1981 is similar: "(The Committee) defined evaluation as the systematic investigation of the worth or merit of some object." According to David Nevo, writing in 1983, considerable consensus has recently been reached with this understanding of evaluation as the "assessment of merit or worth."[10] However, there is another significant strand in the evaluation literature. As indicated above, Cronbach sees the focus of evaluation as the provision of information for decision makers and program improvement. In a major work published in 1980, Cronbach and associates indicate that "by the term evaluation we mean systematic examination of events occurring in and consequent on a contemporary program—an examination conducted to assist in improving this program and other programs having the same general purpose." In the 95 theses on which their call for a "reformation in evaluation" is based, their conception of evaluation as not being directed primarily at judgment is fairly clear, as thesis 12 states: "The hope that an evaluation will provide unequivocal answers, convincing enough to extinguish controversy about the merits of a social program, is certain to be disappointed."[11] Others, such as Robert Stake, Egon Guba and Yvonne Lincoln, hold that evaluation is best understood as both description and assessment of worth.

As many as forty individual models[12] of educational evaluation have appeared in the literature, though most can be categorized into a few basic categories. Of course, many have followed Tyler, using educational objectives as the primary organizer for evaluation; Malcolm Provus' "Discrepancy Model" and W. James Popham's "Instructional Objectives Approach" are significant examples.[13]

In his 1967 "Countenance Model," Robert Stake makes use of the objectives approach and yet makes a considerable advance on Tyler in that he focuses on contextual factors and the educational process as

well as on outcomes. The model calls for two "data matrices," one for description and the other for judgment. Each has two columns, the first being divided into intents and observations and the second into standards and judgment. Both matrices are divided into three rows: antecedents, transactions and outcomes. Thus the evaluator makes entries covering the specified aspects of the program: inputs, process, and outcomes in terms of 1) intentions, 2) the actual conditions observed, and 3) the standards by which discrepancies between intents and observations are to be understood, and 4) interpretations of any discrepancies. It should be recognized that Stake went beyond Tyler not only in specifying a broader area to be examined, but also in that he identified judgment as a specific responsibility of evaluation; that is, evaluation is to go beyond identifying discrepancies between objectives and achievement to explaining or interpreting those discrepancies. The two "countenances" he proposed are those of description and judgment.[14]

The CIPP (Context, Input, Process, Product) model, introduced by Daniel Stufflebeam, provides an example of an approach to evaluation based on the decision situation as the primary organizer. Stufflebeam's primary concern is to provide the information needed for decision making at various points in an educational program. He combined two dimensions, the means-ends and intended-actual, to develop the four stages. Evaluation of context will provide information for objectives and goals, or *intended ends*, while input evaluation, examining various possible processes, provides information for decision making regarding *intended means*. On the other side, process evaluation services *actual means*, and product evaluation provides information about *actual ends* and assists in decision making concerning adjustment, recycling, etc. In each case evaluation can be used to inform decisions still to be made or to evaluate those already made, and in each case the information needed must be identified, obtained, and reported in a manner that will facilitate its application in decision making.[15]

Accreditation studies are among the best known forms of evaluation. Here the advance organizer is the set of guidelines published by the accrediting agency, and the purpose is to determine how the institution or program in question can be improved and whether it meets certain minimum standards, standards which are understood in light of the scope and goals of the institution or program itself. The standards are set by the accrediting agency, which usually consists of a group of professional experts; accreditation has been labeled the "professional-judgment" approach to evaluation. The usual method employed in accreditation is an institutional self-study followed by a visit by a team of experts to verify the findings of the self-study and to gather additional information. In a 1979 speech, Robert Young described the primary accreditation concerns as:

> educational quality, defined and interpreted within the context of the institution or program's statement of its own scope and purpose as compared with similar institutions and programs; and the institutional integrity, viewed from the perspective that the institution or program is what it says it is and does what it says it does educationally at any given point in time.[16]

Accreditation was first developed around the turn of the century, and has gained momentum since the 1930's. Regional accrediting agencies have been established, as have several professional accrediting organizations which focus on specific groups of professional and vocational schools. Accreditation provides an obvious service to the public in its provision of information about specific institutions and programs. On the other hand, it has been criticized for emphasizing intrinsic rather than outcome criteria.[17]

In complete opposition to the objective/achievement model, Michael Scriven put forward education effects as the organizer for evaluation efforts in his "goal-free" model. Having observed that many evaluations turned up positive, though unanticipated, outcomes, and that an arbitrary distinction was usually made between these and the expected outcomes, he recommended in 1974 that no such distinction be made but that all outcomes should be given equal attention. Thus he argued for a goal-free evaluation that would look at actual outcomes rather than at the achievement of a set of objectives, specifying that the evaluator would use a "profile of demonstrated needs in education" to assess these actual outcomes. One of the interesting points made by Scriven's model is the indication that evaluation can take place in the absence of stated objectives.[18]

For the task of developing an evaluation strategy appropriate to nontraditional theological education, the emerging responsive approach, which takes as its primary organizer the "concerns and issues of the stakeholding audiences," may well be the most helpful of the various recent developments in the field. Robert Stake was the first to adopt the term "responsive," a term he uses to indicate an evaluation approach in which the evaluator is more concerned with the interests of the various groups affected by the program being evaluated, groups he calls "stake-

holding audiences," than with the program's stated objectives. Stake recommends the responsive approach as one that

> trades off some measurement precision in order to increase the usefulness of the findings to persons in and around the program . . . An educational evaluation is *responsive evaluation* if it orients more directly to program activities than to program intents; responds to audience requirements for information; and if the different value perspectives present are referred to in reporting the success and failure of the program.[19]

Several different purposes can be served by evaluation, according to Stake; the determination of which purpose is to be served in a given evaluation is based on the concerns and interests of the various audiences present. Thus the proper organizers for an evaluation are the interests of the people around the program, a group which, in a discussion of public education, would include taxpayers, students, parents, administrators, teachers, and others. A distinction can be made between the responsive approach and earlier "preordinate"[20] approaches, a distinction readily understandable from Stake's perspective, particularly in regard to the basis for evaluation design. Others focused primarily on stated objectives, goals, or other hypotheses that were to be tested, while Stake calls for attention to the motivations and problems of the various audiences. Another important distinction between preordinate designs and the responsive approach has to do with the role of the evaluator. In preordinate evaluation, the evaluator is to be objective, external, but in responsive evaluation the evaluator can be drawn into the program and be interactive with the entire process.

As suggested by the dramatic shift in the role of the evaluator, the methods utilized by responsive evaluation are fundamentally different from those used by most preordinate evaluators. The earlier designs follow scientific methods, taking objective readings of phenomena with such instruments as standardized tests. The responsive approach contrasts rather sharply, using methods that are subjective and qualitative and employing tools such as observation and interviews.[21] Further, the evaluator may play an active part in the whole process, negotiating with the various audiences in order to determine the nature of their needs. Responsive evaluation looks to anthropology, ethnography and journalism while earlier preordinate designs look to the methods of experimental psychology, the approaches of the so-called hard sciences, for models and methodological assistance.

Several have contributed to the responsive evaluation approach introduced by Stake; the 1983 collection of essays, *Stakeholder-Based Evaluation*, edited by Anthony Byrk and Graham's "A Rating Scale for Assessing the Quality of Responsive-Illuminative Evaluations"[22] are recent examples. One of the most significant contributions is Guba and Lincoln's *Effective Evaluation: Improving the Usefulness of Evaluation Results Through Responsive and Naturalistic Approaches* which, as the subtitle indicates, links the responsive approach to the use of qualitative methodology. Guba and Lincoln expand Stake's model, defining some of the components more closely, and provide an extensive guide to techniques and skills necessary for the implementation of the approach.

Guba and Lincoln provide helpful definitions for two sets of terms, terms that are fundamental to the interests of the various audiences of an evaluation and to the values on which the evaluation is based. Having established that the appropriate organizers for responsive evaluation are the concerns and issues of the various audiences, "concerns" and "issues" are defined with some precision. "A *concern* is any matter of interest or importance to one or more parties," and might be "any claim, doubt, fear, anticipated difficulty and the like expressed by anyone with a legitimate basis for making such a representation.." Thus examples of concerns would include belief that a program is not meeting its objectives, difficulty in recognizing the relevance of a program to its context, or interest in showing that a new curriculum is better than an existing one. Of course, concerns vary in importance and relevance to a particular evaluation, but none should be dismissed without prior investigation and consideration as a possible focus point. An "issue," on the other hand is "any statement, proposition, or focus that allows for the presentation of different points of view; any proposition about which reasonable persons may disagree; or any point of contention." Examples here would include whether to cut the budget, whether to seek accreditation for a distance education program or whether to involve a particular constituency in a decision making process. Thus, an issue can be any proposition about which there is disagreement between stakeholders.[23] When the broad scope of these concerns and issues of the various audiences is recognized as the appropriate organizer for an evaluation, the shift in attention called for by the responsive approach from a traditional or predetermined set of objectives or values to the interests of those actually affected by the program under evaluation becomes clear.

Guba and Lincoln affirm that, in addition to description, evaluation includes judging the object being evaluated. Here, their assignment of detailed definitions to the terms "merit" and "worth" proves helpful. An entity may have an implicit value, independent of any application or context; to this "intrinsic, context-free value," they apply the term "merit." On the other side, an entity may have value in a particular context, in a practical application; in this "context-determined" situation the term "worth" is applied. Merit maybe be estimated by either assessing the extent to which a program (or some aspect of the program) achieves certain set standards or by comparing the program to a similar one. Worth, on the other hand, has to do with the program's outcomes and impact. Here, the set of requirements by which the program's outcomes are measured are not established by a group of experts (as may be the case in merit determination), but by the local stakeholders who are affected by the program. Thus, the determination of worth is quite variable, depending on the specific context and the audience(s) to which the evaluation is directed.[24]

The attention to a program's "worth," to its practical application in a specific situation and its impact on that situation, is an important aspect of the responsive approach to evaluation, and it fits well with the perception of the primary purpose of evaluation as responding to stakeholder's requirements for information. This attention to the outcomes and impact appears to have important implications for the evaluation of nontraditional education, and for TEE in particular, where greater emphasis is placed on learner outcomes than on procedures and structure.

Endnotes

[1] Virtually all of the journals dedicated to evaluation studies, such as *Educational Evaluation and Policy Analysis, Studies in Educational Evaluation, Evaluation in Education: An International Review, Evaluation Review, Evaluation and Program Planning, Evaluation News,* and *New Directions in Program Evaluation,* have appeared since 1965. For a review of the early history of evaluation see George F. Madaus, Daniel L. Stufflebeam and Michael Scriven, "Program Evaluation: A Historical Overview," in Stufflebeam, *Evaluation Models: Viewpoints on Educational and Human Services Evaluation* (Boston: Kluwer-Nijhoff, 1983) pp. 3-22.

[2] This term is defined in Daniel L. Stufflebeam and William J. Webster, "An Analysis of Alternative Approaches to Evaluation," *Educational Evaluation and Policy Analysis,* 2.3 (May-June 1980): 6, as "the types of variables used to determine information requirements" and "the main cues that evaluators use to set up a study." This concept, by whatever term it is known, is clearly important in developing definitions of evaluation.

[3] Ralph W. Tyler, *Basic Principles of Curriculum and Instruction* (Chicago: University of Chicago Press, 1949), p. 69, a frequently quoted passage.

[4] Egon G. Guba and Yvonne S. Lincoln, *Effective Evaluation: Improving the Usefulness of Evaluation Results through Responsive and Naturalistic Approaches* (San Francisco: Jossey-Bass, 1981), pp. 3-7.

[5] The period before Sputnik, 1946-1957, is labelled the "Age of Innocence" by Madaus, Scriven, and Stufflebeam. This was a period of educational expansion and much building but little call for evaluation. As there was little concern for efficiency or effectiveness. Data were collected, but they were often used to justify expansion and seldom to determine the worth of a program or to improve it. Tyler's methods were widely used, techniques where established in order to define explicit objectives, and taxonomies of the possible educational objectives developed. Bloom's taxonomy is a well known example.

[6] Lee J. Cronbach, "Course Improvement through Evaluation," *Teachers College Record,* 64.8 (May 1963): 672.

[7] Michael Scriven, "The Methodology of Evaluation," *AERA Monograph Series in Curriculum Evaluation,* 1 (1967). Guba and Lincoln, p. 9, indicate that this "deserves to be recognized as the single most important paper on evaluation written to date."

[8] It should be noted that there was no provision made in Tyler's model for evaluating the objectives themselves and thus, according to many evaluators, no provision for such assessing the worth of the program as a whole. Questions such as, On what values are the objectives based? and Whose values are they? are quite important in the stakeholder or responsive approach (which will be discussed below) and in the evaluation of TEE.

[9] Stephen Brookfield, "Evaluation Models and Adult Education," *Studies in Adult Education,* 14 (Sept. 1982): 96.

[10] Daniel L. Stufflebeam, "Evaluation as a Community Education Process," *Community Education Journal,* 5.2 (March-April 1975): 8. Joint Committee on Standards for Educational Evaluation, *Standards for Evaluation of Educational Programs, Projects, and Materials* (New York: McGraw-Hill, 1981), p. 12. David Nevo, "The Conceptualization of Education Evaluation: An Analytical Review of the Literature," *Review of Educational Research,* 53.1 (Spring 1983): 118.

[11] Lee J. Cronbach, et al., *Toward Reform of Program Evaluation: Aims, Methods, and Institutional Arrangements* (San Francisco: Jossey-Bass, 1980), pp. 3, 12.

[12] Some evaluators prefer the terms "approach" or "perspective" to "model." Like many others, I use the terms interchangeably. See Daniel L. Stufflebeam and William J. Webster, "An Analysis of Alternative Approaches to Evaluation," *Educational Evaluation and Policy Analysis,* 2.3 (May-June, 1980): 5-20 and Nevo, "The Conceptualization of Educational Evaluation."

[13] Malcolm Provus, *Discrepancy Evaluation: For Educational Program Improvement and Assessment* (Berkeley: McCutchan, 1971), and W. James Popham, *Educational Evaluation* (Englewood Cliffs: Prentice-Hall, 1975).

[14] Robert E. Stake, "The Countenance of Educational Evaluation," *Teachers College Record,* 68.7 (April 1967): 523-540.

[15] Daniel L. Stufflebeam, et al., *Educational Evaluation and Decision Making* (Itasca, IL: Peacock, 1971). Here I have followed Guba and Lincoln, pages 14-16.

[16] Robert Young, "Evaluating Educational Quality: The Central but changing Role of Accreditation," Keynote address in COPA, *Proceedings: Conference on Assessing Nontraditional Education* (Philadelphia, April 6-7, 1979), ERIC Document ED 182 340.

[17] Stufflebeam and Webster, p. 11, who continue, "the self-study and visitation processes used in accreditation offer many opportunities for corruption and inept performance." On accreditation see: William K. Selden and Harry V. Porter, *Accreditation: Its Purposes and Uses,* (Washington, D. C.: COPA, 1977), and Grover J. Andrews, *A Study of Accreditation in Adult and Continuing Education Programs* (Atlanta: Southern Association of Colleges and Schools, 1973). On self-study, see especially H. R. Kells, *Self-Study Process: a Guide for Postsecondary Institutions* (New York: American Council on Education, 1983, second ed.), and his other work.

18 Michael Scriven, "Goal Free Evaluation," in E. R. House, ed., *School Evaluation: the Politics and Process* (Berkeley: McCutchan, 1973), and Michael Scriven, "Pros and Cons about Goal-Free Evaluation," *Evaluation Comment* 3 (1974): 1-4.

19 Robert E. Stake, *Evaluating the Arts in Education: A Responsive Approach* (Columbus, OH: Merrill, 1975), p. 14, quoted in Guba and Lincoln, p. 24. See also his earlier essay, written with C. Gjerde, "An Evaluation of CITY, The Twin City Institute for Talented Youth," in Richard H. P. Kraft, ed., *Four Evaluation Examples: Anthropological, Economic, Narrative, and Portrayal* (Chicago: Rand McNally, 1974), pp. 99-139, which covers the study in which he began to formulate the responsive approach. He adopted this new posture following his work on the countenance model which was mentioned above.

20 Guba and Lincoln, pp. 27-33.

21 This shift toward qualitative methodology is receiving a great deal of attention in the literature. See Eileen Kuhn and S. V. Mortorana, eds., *Qualitative Methods for Institutional Research* (San Francisco: Jossey-Bass, 1982); John van Maanen, ed., *Qualitative Methodology* (Beverly Hills: Sage, 1983); Matthew B. Miles and A. Michael Huberman, *Qualitative Data Analysis: A Sourcebook of New Methods* (Beverly Hills: Sage, 1984); and Michael Quinn Patton, *Qualitative Evaluation Methods* (Beverly Hills: Sage, 1980). It appears that neither quantitative nor qualitative methodology is upper-most in popularity, but as most evaluators indicate, different methods are appropriate in different situations and no one approach is the best for every question in every evaluation.

22 Anthony S. Bryk, *Stakeholder-Based Evaluation* (San Francisco: Jossey-Bass, 1983), and Graham S. Maxwell, "A Rating Scale for Assessing the Quality of Responsive-Illuminative Evaluations," *Educational Evaluation and Program Analysis*, 6.2 (Summer 1984): 131-138.

23 Guba and Lincoln, pp. 33-35.

24 Guba and Lincoln, pp. 39-52.

Community-Based Evaluation

A Process Appropriate for Theological Education by Extension

A survey of the values held by TEE advocates reveals significant similarities around the world. The same basic commitments exist in virtually every program—commitments to training in context, to the selection of students by local churches, to dialogue between students and tutors, and to providing service to a particular community. These perspectives lead to an evaluation approach centered on the community being served by the extension program considering evaluation. "Community-based" evaluation suggests that an individual TEE program might best evaluate its life and work in light of the values, concerns, and interests of the community it serves. A brief review of TEE perspectives, along with the recently developed responsive approach in educational program evaluation, will provide an indication of the value a community approach to evaluation has for TEE programs.

A commitment to the context of present and future ministry as the best location for training is shared by all TEE programs. Rather than removing students from their local churches, from the responsibilities and experiences related to their home communities, extension accepts these experiences as appropriate and valuable channels for learning. The student is immersed in the business of daily life and is encouraged to evaluate the academic study material from the viewpoint of daily realities. Training in context provides the possibility of relating theoretical input directly to the specific needs of the student and of the situation in which the student is, and will be, ministering. Many TEE advocates call for programs and course materials to be shaped by the context of the student and the ministry situation; the realities of the people served by the extension program must form the basis for the content and methods of the program itself. The implications here for an evaluation approach based on the input of the community served are fairly clear. If context is to play the determining role in designing extension programs, it follows that the evaluation of these programs should be centered on the same, specific context.

Another widely held TEE perspective is that the location of authority in the student selection should be in the local church rather than in the educational institution. As leadership formation and selection most frequently take place within the potential lead-er's society, TEE programs usually recognize the local church/community as the most appropriate context for the identification of potential students. Again, support for a community-based approach to evaluation should be clear. If the local community is recognized as possessing the ability to identify those who can best serve in a specific context, it should also be recognized as a primary resource in the evaluation process.

Open, equal communication is an ideal that is found nearly everywhere in TEE. Center leaders are to learn alongside students, helping them reach their own conclusions, rather than to lecture and impose information. Seminars are to be opportunities for exchange between co-learners who share common goals. Recognition of students as adults comes in here, another point accepted throughout TEE. Adults bring experience of the field to be studied as well as experience of life and so have a valuable basis for interaction with the study material and with other learners. The maturity of students is often stressed; they are able to participate in all aspects of the learning process and have a full understanding of their own needs and those of the people they are, and will be, serving. The learning situation for a TEE student is often an immediate problem or specific situation in the church or surrounding community. Students are obviously key members of the community served by an educational program and should be recognized as having important contributions to make both in the learning process and in the decision making relating to the whole program. If TEE is accepted as adult education in which dialogue and open communication are at the center, it is fairly clear that students should have important input for any evaluation process.

The concepts of leadership through service, of modeling servanthood, and of the theological education institution as the servant of a specific community are common to many TEE programs. These conceptions of service are particularly important for the recognition of the centrality of the community being served by an extension program in any evaluation of that program. Recognizing the servant relationship between the TEE program and the community, whether that community is defined as consisting of the members of a single denomination, of several religious groups, or of all members of society in a certain geographical area, it is clear that input on goals and assessment from the community is necessary. Service can begin with acceptance of the community members' perceptions of training needs rather than offering predefined curricula and procedures. It might include not only a program designed to meet those needs, but also readiness to ask the members of the community if service is actually being provided. TEE programs that exist to serve a specific community can only benefit from the evaluation related input of community members.

Recognition of the variations that exist between TEE programs provides another rationale for basing evaluation on the needs and desires of the specific community served by the program in question. Some programs support a conception of ministry by all and provide training for laity only or for laity alongside those going forward to ordination. Others see their purpose solely in the preparation of clergy. There is a wide diversity in theological stances among TEE programs; some are particularly concerned with evangelism and church planting while others have an additional deep commitment to the needs of society and hope to train leaders who will combine Christian ministry with service in the local community. The understanding of TEE as a force for liberation can be found in some communities, but many others see extension primarily as a method by which more pastors can be trained for traditional ministry. The extension side of TEE also varies; many programs provide access to students who were formerly excluded from training opportunities because of race, sex, financial ability, or previous academic achievement, while others concentrate on geographical extension, offering classes at times when employed persons can attend. An evaluation format that would require this variety of programs to meet a single set of externally established standards could hardly be as helpful for basic program improvement as a format designed to assist each program in meeting the needs of its own community.

In the recent deluge of evaluation literature, strong support is provided for a community-based format by the "responsive" approach which emphasizes the concerns and interests of "stakeholders." These stakeholders are identified as all of the various groups affected by the program being evaluated. Evaluation is to be responsive to the needs of the people around the education program in question, accepting their concerns and dealing with any differences of opinions held by members of the affected audiences. Thus the concerns and issues of the people affected by the education program provide the organizers the material on which the evaluation is to be based. The shift away from traditional, predefined standards as the center of an evaluation to the con-

cerns of the people actually affected by the program being evaluated called for in the responsive approach has important significance for the evaluation of TEE. The responsive approach allows the values of the community being served by the extension program, values which are often determined by the Bible, by the needs of the community, or by the special interests of a specific group, to form the center of the evaluation rather than traditional or other, possibly unrelated, values to establish standards.

The responsive approach emphasizes methods that are qualitative rather than quantitative, using interviews and observation. The evaluator may become involved in the process, dialoguing with various participants and stakeholders. In another development in evaluation research, recent studies indicate that increased involvement by program participants in the evaluation process not only assists in collecting the needed information but also enhances the eventual use of evaluation results.

A community-based approach to evaluation for TEE must begin with gathering information from all who are affected by the program. This group will normally consist not only of students, center leaders, and TEE administrators, but also graduates of the program, local pastors and lay people, and possibly even those members of the larger society the program wishes to serve. The input of this group is especially important for evaluation because it has the potential of representing every aspect of the service provided by the training program. "Community" seems to be the most appropriate term for this group because of the connection it provides with the Christian idea of *koinonia*, in which members participate in the needs of each other, and with the Body of Christ, in which the full involvement of all parts is required. The concerns and issues expressed by those served, either directly or indirectly, by the program, alongside the input of the center leaders, program administrators, and supporters, provide the foundation for the evaluation.

Basing an evaluation process on the concerns and objectives expressed by the specific community served by the program under evaluation indicates a major shift away from traditional approaches in which an institution determines whether it is meeting "standards" set either by an external group of professionals or by its own administration or governing board. Community-based evaluation, on the other hand, focuses on the extent to which the objectives of a specific community are being met.

Gathering information relating to the various aspects of the program from the members of the served community is clearly a difficult and time consuming process but one which should have several benefits in addition to the provision of the basis for evaluation. The simple business of talking with, and learning from, the many parts of the whole church/community affected by the TEE program is valuable in itself. All will be allowed to participate and so to take ownership. This process of dialogue has implications for enrollments, for the acceptance of TEE graduates, and for increased communication among the members of the community.

The suggested evaluation process is divided into three parts: community input, descriptive self-study, and assessment. These three stages provide a framework in which a TEE program might gather information from the community it serves, state specific objectives and describe the related educational processes, and assess the manner in which processes and outcomes relate to the community's stated values and concerns. Each of the three stages is divided into nine "areas" that cover every aspect of a TEE program: mission, access, program content, educational process, center leaders, text materials, relations with the local church/community, planning-administration-finances, and impact.

The input gathered from the community in the first stage forms the basis for the evaluation, for the statements of objectives and for the assessment. The process is best thought of in terms of dialogue, of mutual communication, in which all (or as many as possible) participate in sharing needs, concerns, and interests. Openness, readiness to listen (even to the unexpected), is required throughout. Of course, dialogue should not be strictly controlled or limited to specific areas; unexpected topics and input should be expected. Though many variations of the process are possible, it should be recognized that the worth of the evaluation to the community will increase as more community members participate.

In the second part of the evaluation process, the information gathered from the community provides the primary resource for a "statement of objectives" in each of the nine areas. These objectives may provide a concise, clear statement of the response to the questions earlier presented to the whole community, and/or may reflect the special concerns of the team conducting the evaluation, the program administrators, or the supporting body. Obviously, at this point special care must be taken to insure that the concerns and interests of the community are fairly presented. Members of the evaluation team (hopefully, themselves representative of the diversity of the community served), TEE administrators, and other church officials are members of the whole community and should participate fully in the dialogue relat-

ing to the establishment of objectives, but from a position of service, not domination. A description of the area of the program designed to meet each objective can then be prepared. These self-descriptions provide both a report on the current structures, curriculum, student and center leader profiles, etc., and also an indication of the correspondence with the related community input.

Assessment via outcomes is an appropriate component of the evaluation of TEE programs, especially where desired outcomes are specified by the community served. Thus the third part of the evaluation provides for an assessment in each area of the extent to which the stated objectives (representing the community's concerns and issues, if accepted by the evaluation team) are actually being met, though not all of the nine areas specifically treat learner outcomes. In each area there may also be an indication of proposed changes, recommendations for improvement, or suggestions for bringing a specific aspect into closer correlation with the desires of the community.

An evaluation based on community needs and concerns will be best conducted by a team of representatives of the community itself. Before such an evaluation team can be selected, however, the community served by the program under evaluation must be defined with some care. With the term "community" defined as all who are affected by the program, the groups of people served, both directly (such as students) and indirectly (such as pastors and lay people), and all other interested persons (such as administrators and supporters) can be described. The evaluation team, then, might well be made up of at least one representative of every group served by the TEE program.

Theological foundations for a community-based approach to evaluation are readily found in some of the basic New Testament themes, themes that are often reflected in the TEE literature and have to do with service and servanthood, *koinonia* among members of the Christian community, and the nature of the community itself.

Paul's conception of the Body of Christ as consisting of various members each with certain gifts forms the foundation for many TEE programs designed to develop those gifts for use in Christian service. In his presentation of the Christian community as one body in I Corinthians 12, Paul describes the body as having many members, each with gifts, and declares emphatically that none of the members can be dismissed or ignored without dysfunction in the whole. In fact, those members that appear to be the unimportant or less significant ones he singles out for special notice; "the parts of the body which seem to be weaker are indispensable." A similar point is made in Ephesians 4; bodily growth is possible when *each* part is working properly. The implication here for the participation by all within the community are quite clear; the model consists of interdependent members, each with a valuable contribution to the well being of the whole body.

Related to the idea of the Body of Christ in which all parts are needed, Paul uses the term *koinonia* to illustrate the manner and quality of relationships within the body. As is well known, the term does multiple duty in Paul's writing, referring to the fellowship of the believer with Christ and to the participation in Christ that takes place at the Lord's Supper as well as to the relations that should hold among members of the Christian community. Communion with Christ is to issue in the mutual fellowship (communion, sharing, participation) of members of the community, a mutuality that at times extends to participating in the physical needs of others. Mutual assistance, sharing, and openness to full participation, which are to characterize relationships in the Christian community, provide foundations for the dialogue that is at the center of the community-based approach to evaluation.

References to Jesus' example of service and selfless giving and to his presentation of leadership as servanthood are found frequently in the TEE literature. Extension programs often present statements of mission in terms of service, and servanthood, a primary objective of character development, is to be modeled in relations both with students and with the whole community. Support from Jesus' life and teaching is unmistakable; he instructs his disciples not to follow the example of leaders who dominate those they rule over but rather the model of Jesus himself (Mark 10.43 ff). Paul echoes this call to servanthood in imitation of Christ in his well-known passage in Philippians 2: "Have this mind among yourselves, which you have in Christ Jesus, who . . . emptied himself, taking the form of a servant."

Recognizing that TEE programs usually exist in order to serve a particular community, and understanding servanthood as the approach to leadership advocated in the New Testament, evaluation based on dialogue with the members of that community, asking those being served if service is actually being provided, only follows. Service and servanthood are primary perspectives found in virtually all TEE programs, perspectives with unmistakable roots in the Christian tradition and, especially, in the example of Jesus himself.

TEE Evaluation Workbook

PART 1: COMMUNITY INPUT

For each of the following areas, gather information from the various members of the community that the TEE program serves. Through communication methods appropriate to your own situation, explore each objective area in order to gain a clear understanding of the educational needs, desires, and perceptions of students, tutors, lay people, pastors, graduates and others affected by the program. This is a critically important aspect of the evaluation process and may take considerable time and effort. Notice that the objectives called for in Part 2 should not be written until the information from the community is available.

Each Area in Part 1 contains a short, general question and several discussion questions to help introduce more specific aspects. Each Area also has a set of questions designed to assist in finding ways to determine when a particular objective has been accomplished. This last section is designed by an "A" following the Part and Area number.

1.1 Mission

- What should be the primary goal of the TEE program?

- How should the overall mission of the TEE program be understood? What is the need in your church and/or community that the TEE program should be meeting? Is there a lack of ordained pastors or lay leaders, a need for theological education among the laity, a need for training in community related skills, or some other need that the TEE program should address? Are there values (such as academic excellence, spiritual and character development, contextualization, relevance of studies to experiences of the members of the community, or others) that should be evident throughout the program?

1.1A How will we know if the mission is being accomplished? What question will the community ask (in one year and in five years) in order to determine whether or not the TEE program has been successful in its mission?

1.2 Access

- Who should the students be?

- Should the student body be restricted to ordination candidates, pastors needing retraining, prospective lay leaders, church teachers, counselors, community social and health workers, all church people, only college graduates, only secondary school graduates, only primary school graduates, only men or women, only mature adults, only those recommended by the local church, only those recommended by the denomination officials, to some other group, or should it be open to anyone who wishes training? What should the program do to be as available as possible to the specified potential students? What entrance requirements, if any, should be maintained? Should there be any exceptions to these requirements? Should different programs for different kinds of students be offered, or should all study together if there are students at different levels or with different goals?

1.2A How will we know that the program is actually accessible to this specified group of students? By what criteria should the accessibility of the TEE program be measured? If the program is primarily for ordination candidates (or some other specified group), should a limit be set on the number of non-ordination candidates who are permitted to enroll?

1.3 Program Content

- What should be taught?

- Should the emphasis be placed on academic knowledge, practical ministerial and leadership skills, spiritual and character formation, on all of these, or on some others? What areas should receive primary attention: Biblical, theological, and historical studies, Biblical languages, pastoral skills in preaching, teaching, counseling, community and primary health work, liberal arts knowledge, social analysis skills, research, or on other subject and skill areas? How should the academic, practical, and spiritual formation sides be related or integrated? Should separate programs be offered at different academic levels? (The evaluation team may wish to provide copies of the present curriculum, the possible or proposed variations, and ask for responses and suggestions.)

1.3A How will we determine if the specified subjects and skills have been learned? What is an acceptable or adequate level of learning? Should a determination of success be based on academic

examinations, on oral discussion of studied topics, on practical ministry achievements, on preaching skills, or on some other measurement?

1.4 Educational Process

- How should the program's academic content, practical skills, and concern for spiritual formation be presented to the students? What is the best educational process?

- Do students benefit more from training in an academic and/or spiritual community somewhat removed from day-to-day pressures of jobs and other responsibilities or from part-time training in their usual contexts? Would these students learn better by studying on their own or in groups? What are the benefits, if any, of undertaking an educational program while continuing in a secular job and in church related responsibilities?

- If extension is accepted as an appropriate process (given the constraints of students' other responsibilities, the values of studying in context, the lack of financial and other resources): What should the total length of the course(s) be? What emphasis should be placed on learning and sharing with other students? How often should seminars meet? How often should all the students from the geographical regions and from the whole program meet together? What should the priority of the seminars be? Should they focus on teaching/lecturing, discussion of academic material, sharing experiences, or something else? How should spiritual and character formation be approached? (The evaluation team may wish to offer a description of the existing process with its various components alongside a presentation of other theological education formats—such as residence, short-term courses, and correspondence—with the benefits and problems of each.)

1.4A How will we know if the established process is appropriate? Should the determination of success in the educational process be established by the measures designated by 1.4A? Are there other suggestions?

1.5 Center Leaders

- How should center leaders be selected and what characteristics should they possess?

- Should center leaders (tutors, seminar leaders, facilitators, etc.) have special training for the position? Should they have experience, or presently be serving, as a pastor? Should they have a certain level of formal theological training? Should they be understood as spiritual as well as academic models for the students, or is the idea of a model inappropriate? What role should leaders play in the seminar meetings? Should they lecture, lead discussions, or serve only as organizers, administrators, and encourage students to do all the talking?

1.5A How will we know if the specifications relating to center leaders are being met? If, for example, the characteristic of "discussion leader" is agreed on, should that characteristic—of leading others to speak and to share their own ideas—be looked for only in the center leader, or also in the students who have studied with that leader? To what extent should the reports of students be used in evaluating center leaders?

1.6 Text Materials

- What kinds of text materials should be used?

- Should the students spend their time reading materials prepared by writers from the specific program in question (or denomination, country, or other geographical area) or "standard" textbooks, whether originally written locally or in other parts of the world?

- Is there a need for printed learning resources beyond the self-study materials provided with individual courses?

- Comments and suggestions on programmed materials, workbooks, textbooks, and other forms of printed instructional materials might also be sought.

1.6A How will we know if we are using the best possible texts for our students in our situation? Should the students, graduates, local pastors, tutors, or someone else make this decision?

1.7 Relations with the Local Church/Community

- How should the TEE program be related to the local churches and/or to the local community?

- To what extent should TEE students and tutors be involved in the life of the church? To what extent should they also be involved in service to the larger community? Should this involvement in church and community be left up to the individual student and tutor or should it be required as part of the course? What part should church/community work play in the total TEE program? Should performance in church/community work be part of the student's evaluation? Are you, as an individual church/community person, willing to help in the supervision and evaluation of students?

- How should churches be involved in TEE? Should the local church be responsible for providing information about TEE to prospective students, supplying facilities for seminar meetings, supporting the work of students, and helping with student supervision and evaluation?

1.7A How will we know when the two-way relationship between the TEE program and the local churches and community is at the best level possible? How should a student's work in the church and in the community be evaluated? Should this be the job of the local pastor, community leaders, lay persons, or someone else?

1.8 Planning, Administration, And Finances

- Who should participate in planning and decision making?

- To whom does the program belong? Who is responsible for the program? Should the group responsible for planning and making decisions be limited to the denomination and program administrators? Should it also include pastors, students, tutors, and/or lay and community people? Should it consist of a small group representing the whole, or of some other group of people?

- Should the program be financed by the local churches, by the students, by foreign funding agencies, or by some other means? What percentage of the costs should be the responsibility of the students? Will funding by foreign sources lead to external control?

1.8A How will success in this area be determined? How will it be established that a single individual or group does not control the design and operation of the TEE program to the exclusion of other affected groups? How can we establish that the program is administered with integrity and honesty? How can we determine that the level of costs borne by students, local churches, and others is not overburdening?

1.9 Impact

- What impact should the program have on students, churches, the surrounding community, and other theological education institutions?

- What total effect should the program have on students who go through the courses? What should they know, what skills should they have, what characteristics should their lives illustrate? How should they perform as pastors, lay leaders, or community workers? (There may be some overlap here with areas already covered, such as 1.1, 1.3, and 1.4)

- Should the church change, grow, or shift emphasis in some way as a result of the TEE program? What benefit should parishioners receive if their pastor has undertaken TEE studies? What impact, if any, should be expected in the surrounding community?

1.9A How can we determine if the program is having the specified impact? Is church growth a significant indicator? Is the opinion of the surrounding community valuable in determining the success of the TEE program? Should we look for new churches being established, or for new schools or health centers?

How can we determine if the program has had the desired impact on students? How should they preach, teach, or display other pastoral skills? How should their new knowledge and new skills be measured? What level of knowledge and skills is adequate? Should the TEE program put time and effort into tracking graduates over a period of time in order to determine what and how they are doing after they leave the program? Should the measure of the graduates' success be concentrated on knowledge, spiritual growth or practical abilities?

PART 2: DESCRIPTIVE SELF-STUDY

For each of the following Areas, state objectives and prepare descriptions of your existing program. The "statement of objective" calls for a succinct response to the question posed in the corresponding Area in Part 1. "Description" calls for an account of the way in which your program is attempting to meet the objective.

Community Questions

1. What should be the primary goal of the TEE program?

2. Who should the students be?

3. What should be taught?

4. How should the program's academic content, practical skills, and concern for spiritual formation be presented to the students? What is the best educational process?

5. How should center leaders be selected and what characteristics should they possess?

6. What kinds of text materials should be used?

7. How should the TEE program be related to the local churches and to the local community?

8. Who should participate in planning and decision making?

9. What impact should the program have on students, churches and the surrounding community?

2.1 Mission

Statement of Mission:

Write the mission statement using the values, needs and concerns indicated by the whole community as guidelines. The mission statement (or statement of purpose) provides an encompassing declaration of the intention of the institution. The statement might include a statement of faith and other values that underlie the specific objectives of the institution, especially as they relate to the community that is being served, the selection of students, and the program of study. The objectives called for in the following Areas provide the specifics of the mission statement, and the descriptions in those Areas should indicate the way the program has been developed to accomplish the stated mission.

2.2 Access

Statement of Objective:

State the objective in the light of the community's input, defining the characteristics of all the students for whom your program is designed, distinguishing, if appropriate, between the various courses offered. If availability to nontraditional students (or groups of students described in another way) is a priority, you may wish to state that commitment. You may also wish to define the way in which access to your extension program is different from access to a residential program.

Description:

- Describe the program's entrance requirements, distinguishing, if appropriate, between levels. Do students come at will or only upon recommendation of their churches?

- Describe recruitment and application procedures.

- Describe the student body, giving details of age, sex, academic background, marital status, previous church/community service or involvement, and academic and professional/vocational goals.

- Describe efforts taken to prevent discrimination in student selection.

2.3 Program Content

Statement of Objective:

Write the objective in the light of the community's input, describing what students should know, what skills they should possess, and/or what spiritual or character growth should be evident when the course is completed. State the intended relationship between academic, practical, and character formation emphases and any guiding principles for developing curriculum.

Description:

- Describe the academic curriculum of the program, distinguishing between levels as appropriate. For each course of study (certificate, diploma, or other designation) list the courses offered and the requirements for completion. For each course provide a brief description, including the titles of texts used, prerequisites (if any), and other related data.

- Describe the practical work, church responsibilities, and/or community service, and give details of the method of supervision and evaluation. What emphasis is given to practical skills in student performance evaluation?

2.4 Educational Process

Statement of Objective:

Write the objective in the light of the community's input, stating the reasons for selecting an extension format for theological education and indicating how issues such as training in context, self-study, dialogue, and on-going church/community service is viewed.

Description:

- Describe the way the material outlined in 2.3 is covered.

- Explain the roles of home-study, seminar meetings, and church/community involvement as appropriate.

- Explain the correspondence between the educational process being used and the overall mission of the TEE program.

2.5 Center Leaders

Statement of Objective:

Write the objective in the light of the community's response to the question, "How should tutors be selected and what characteristics should they possess?" You may wish to state the program's objectives regarding the training of tutors and required or recommended experience and characteristics.

Description:

- Describe the process by which center leaders are selected and the characteristics that are considered important for them to possess. Are center leaders to be role models? Describe the leadership tech-

niques that are recommended for seminar meetings.

- Provide a profile of present center leaders, giving information regarding experience, education, and any other data considered relevant. Describe the relationship between center leaders and students.

- Describe the training program for center leaders, if any.

2.6 Text Materials

Statement of Objectives:

Write the objective in light of the community's input, describing the characteristics of text materials that are considered ideal for your program. You may wish to state your objectives relating to origin, format, academic level, and theological and/or ideological perspectives.

Description:

- Describe the text materials being used, including illustrations of format, discussion of academic level(s), and auxiliary reading if any.

- Describe your text selection process, explaining how publishers and individual titles are approved. If some texts are produced locally and others imported, describe the relationship between the two, and how you arrived at it.

- As appropriate, describe text production, provision for training writers, and projections for future text production.

- Describe any other learning resources that are available to extension students.

- Explain the correspondence between the description of the text materials being used and the overall mission of the program.

2.7 Relations with the Local Church/Community

Statement of Objective:

Write the objective in the light of the community's input, stating the reciprocal relations that should exist between the TEE program and the local churches and/or the local community.

Description:

- Describe the involvement of students (and tutors) in the life of the local churches and the local community.

- Describe the support provided by the churches and/or the community, including the provision of facilities, assistance with student supervision and evaluation, and any other participation in the program.

2.8 Planning, Administration, and Finances

Statement of Objectives:

Write the objective by defining those individuals and groups who should control the program and stating the values and practices that should be evident in its operation, using the input of the community as a guideline.

Description:

- Describe the governance structure, indicating lines of responsibility and communication. Describe the planning process, for both immediate and long-range goals, by explaining how decisions are made in each of the major areas and by listing the individuals and groups participating at each point.
- Describe the administration practices, indicating the communication links between central and regional centers, tutors and students.
- Describe the record keeping process.
- Describe the way in which the program is publicized and the efforts that are made to insure that students are not misled.
- Describe the funding and budget processes for the entire program and the prospects for long-term economic stability.
- Explain the financial load carried by the students, indicating student fees, methods of collecting fees, and the process for providing refunds.

2.9 Impact

Statement of Objective:

Write the objective in light of the community's input and the overall mission, stating the effect the program should have on students, churches and the surrounding communities.

PART 3: ASSESSMENT

Part 3 provides for an assessment of the extent to which the values and concerns indicated in Part 1 and (if accepted by the evaluation team) stated in the objectives of Part 2 are being achieved. Any information gathered from the A sections in Part 1 should be used to supplement and, where appropriate, redesign the suggestions for assessment presented here. Indicated changes and projected improvements should also be reported for each Area.

3.1 Mission

- How does the statement of mission correspond to the values, wishes, and concerns of the community as indicated in 1.1?

- If there are significant differences between the mission statement and the community's values, how are these differences explained? What are the reasons behind the adoption of an overall mission that is at variance with the wishes and concerns of the community?
- Describe the way in which the needs of the church, of its leadership, and of the community have been examined to lead the writers of the mission statement to an understanding of the specific situation or problem that must be addressed. How did you arrive at the description of the job to be done?
- Does the existing statement of mission meet the approval of the current students, governing board, graduates, center leaders, administrators, and other interested groups affected by the program?

3.2 Access

- How does the student body profile (giving the various characteristics of all students in each course of study) correspond to the values and objectives indicated by the whole community in relation to student selection?
- Indicate the changes proposed, if any, in the student population.

3.3 Program Content

- Has the subject matter identified in 1.3 and 2.3 been learned by students who have completed the program? How have their learning achievement levels been measured?
- What ministerial skills and indications of spiritual growth do graduates possess? Do these skills and indications correspond to the value specified by the community as required of graduates? How has the presence or absence of practical skills and spiritual development been determined.
- How do parishioners evaluate the training of pastors who have gone through the extension program? Are graduates considered "successful" in the ministry for which they are prepared through the TEE program by other members of the whole community?
- What do students, graduates, and center leaders say about the existing curriculum?
- If changes are suggested, how and when will they be implemented?

3.4 Educational Process

- Does the description of the process (2.4) correspond to the educational values indicated by the community and the stated objective (1.4)?

- What do students, graduates, and local pastors say about the extension format?
- If it is considered helpful and appropriate, you may wish to compare student outcomes from the extension program to those from a residential school or other programs employing a different format. This comparison might be based on examination results, length and nature of involvement in Christian ministry after graduation, evaluation of graduates by parishioners and other members of the community, or on some other scale.
- If changes are suggested for any of the components of the extension program, how and when will they be implemented?

3.5 Center Leaders

- How does the profile of center leaders correspond to the values indicated by the community relating to leadership, training, role modeling, and other characteristics.
- How do students evaluate center leaders?
- How do center leaders evaluate themselves, their need for training or other qualification, and the existing training and/or qualification process?
- How do local pastors and other interested members of the community evaluate center leaders?
- If changes are suggested in center leader training or selection, how and when will they be made?

3.6 Text Materials

- How do the text materials presently in use correspond to the values of the community and the objectives for texts?
- How do students and center leaders evaluate the existing texts?
- If changes are suggested, how and when will they be made?

3.7 Relations with the Local Church/Community

- Does the level of student participation in the life and work of the churches and in the surrounding community meet the expectations indicated in 1.7?
- Is the support received by the TEE program from the churches and the community adequate? Is the

level of supervision provided by the local pastors and other community leaders for students in church and community work adequate?
- If there are variations in the expected and actual mutual relations between the TEE program and the churches and/or community, how and when will the needed improvements be introduced?

3.8 Planning, Administration, and Finances

- Do the ways in which planning and governance take place involve those groups specified by the community as responsible for these roles? How do the various groups that make up the whole community view their individual involvement in planning and control of the program?
- If funding is provided by external sources, is there evidence that control is also distant from the program?
- If the program is externally controlled and this is at variance with the wishes of the whole community, what measures are being taken to establish local control?
- Is there an existing process for planning for the future?
- Is the TEE program administered with honesty and integrity and/or other values indicated as necessary by the whole community? What is the evidence of these characteristics?
- Describe any proposed changes in the planning and administration structure.

3.9 Impact

- How do the various individuals affected by the program, including lay people, pastors, local community leaders, students, graduates, center leaders, and TEE administrators, evaluate its total impact?
- What evidence is there that the TEE program has an impact on surrounding institutions, including churches, health and education projects, and other aspects of the community?
- How does the impact of the TEE program correspond to its mission? Is the program accomplishing what it set out to do?

Accreditation and Theological Education

John Hanson in his book *Imagination and Hallucination in African Education* has dramatically posed the problem of accreditation as it appears in African education. It is between *équivalence* (or European Standards) and *negritude* (or Africanization). African educators fear that their programs will be viewed as of "lower stature" or "watered down," that is, of less value than their European counterparts. Thus, since centralized examinations are used to "maintain standards," vocational students in certain countries in the tropics are expected to master the "syllabus of 'the city and guilds of London,' resulting in such phenomena as students building European style fireplaces in the 120 degree F heat of Khartoum, Sudan." Can education that is not the same as be as-good-as some other education?

This conflict has been faced a number of times in the history of the Christian church. The first time the Apostle Peter had to face up to the problem of as-good-as was when the Holy Spirit manifested in Cornelius and his family the gifts of Pentecost. Another notable confrontation occurred at the Reformation, when the Eucharist could be celebrated without a priest, and again in early Methodism, when ordination took place without an officially recognized bishop. There have been many others. Today it must be faced in theological education. Historically those who have stood for standards have had to give way to those who stood for relevance, who in their turn developed new standards.

Two methods are in use to guarantee as-good-as education: centralized, standardized examinations and institutional accreditation. The European systems, whether of the English or French model, have relied on the standard, authorized examinations. Where all students study the same material and submit to the same examinations there is no real problem of equivalence. With these systems of education, the problem is the practical value of education, relevance. Does it prepare people to contribute as citizens of their country, or does it make them aliens and ill adapted to any but Western societies?

In the U. S. A. accreditation was invented, and it has been spreading over the globe. It grew out of a situation very like that of theological education worldwide today, and especially similar to the situation with extension theological education. During the later part of the nineteenth century there was a tremendous growth in the number of schools at the secondary and college levels in the U. S. A. Following the expansion of the population from the eastern seaboard to the Pacific coast in some 50 years, the settlers started schools. As large numbers of the settlements were composed of distinct religious groups, most of the institutions were church related. The question arose, how is it possible to tell if a student from school A has the background to enter college B? Associations of secondary schools and colleges were formed to assure equivalence. They desired to impose minimum standards on secondary schools for entrance into college, and also to provide a way to evaluate equivalence for transfer students. Being accredited also became important in order to establish credibility with the supporting constituencies, that is, to raise funds to support the school. After initial accreditation, standards were maintained or improved in most institutions. To become accredited was important only for new and marginal schools in order for them to be accepted and for their students to be able to transfer to other institutions. As a result, the attention of the associations turned from accrediting schools to improving the quality of existing institutions.

In the case of Theological Education by Extension (TEE) it had been judged by many as inferior to the residential pattern from the very beginning. In Guatemala, where the experiment began, the seminary students and graduates appear to have formed an image taken from what they understood to have been the missionaries' experience. It was assumed that the missionaries had attended residence schools where classes were held during the day; this then must be the way things should be done if our education is to be as-good-as theirs. Much of the early writing on extension was a defense of the changes, trying to demonstrate that it was as-good-as residential training, even though decentralized and evening schools were well accepted for the national university and secondary schools. As Frank Abbot observed, "changing the curriculum entails all the physical and psychological difficulties of moving a cemetery." (1985:5) In this case, not only the list of courses was being changed, but the curriculum, the teaching methods, the locale, the kind of students, everything was being altered.

TEE was an effort to return to some of the values of an apprenticeship. Referring to specialized knowledge and theoretical understanding,

These are presumably taught most efficiently in professional schools rather than through apprenticeship or trial and error. Yet it is by no means easy to adduce empirical evidence in support of this seemingly self-evident presumption. On the contrary, the available evidence suggests that what seems to be self-evident may well be quite untrue. (Jenks & Riesman 1968:205)

Standardization was early proposed for extension, not by accreditation but by a standard curriculum with accompanying texts. (For details see Winter 1969) Four levels were created corresponding to a person's previous studies: literate, primary, secondary, and university secular education. The program was never carried out as originally planned, though the names of some of the levels have taken root. With the spread worldwide of extension systems, the divergence of programs ranging from the semiliterates of Honduras to those offering doctorates have appeared. (Kinsler 1981) A wide diversity of materials has also appeared, written from different points of view and within different cultures. The issue of equivalence in this confusing situation has again been posed.

The purpose of this paper is to examine some of the critical issues related to accreditation and to raise the question of its value for the church and its institutions. In order to establish equivalence, to show that one type of education is as-good-as another implies that some type of measurement must be made and then compared. Finally a value judgment must be made about the comparison: is it as good as others, or as it should be? Let us first examine the problem of measurement and evaluation.

Evaluation

Evaluation of education is carried out continuously and often at more than one level. The educational process, and the points at which assessment and evaluation might be carried out can be visualized in the diagram.

In all educational systems there are ideals of what a graduate should know, be, or be able to do. These are defined in some way and practically specified in some series of units of study or practices and experiences. There is some expected entry level of understanding and ability required for prospective students. The first comparison is made between the abilities expected and what the students actually have. Frequently the proposed entry level does not correspond to what students actually bring, and often the entry requirements restrict the potential student group to an inappropriate population. That is to say, only people who are not presently leaders in the churches might meet the requirements, or people who are mature and responsible might not have the educational prerequisites required.

Other comparisons can be made between what an institution proposes (the ideal) and what actually occurs in the program. As in the following diagram, these comparisons can be made at the course level, as a final examination or relative to the progress the student has made. The institution as a whole may be compared with external standards for accreditation.

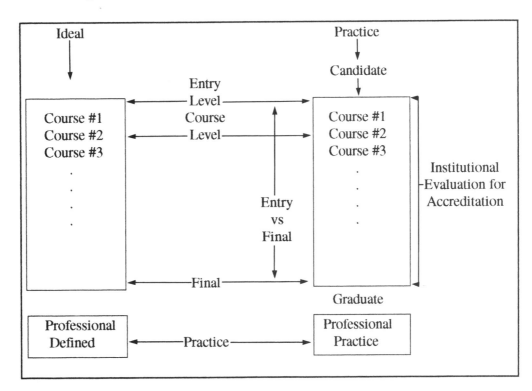

Another comparison is made where licensing is separate from the school, at the professional level. In churches, this usually consists of examinations for ordination by a church body separate from the school. This is the real test, whether the graduate can in practice exhibit the qualities, attitudes, activities that exemplify the ministry. In only one case was an effort made to accredit schools on the basis of later practice. This study related to students' success in graduate school on the basis of their undergraduate studies. There was so much opposition to the study that the results were suppressed, thus ending the experiment. (Seldon 1960:46) The problems of evaluation are complicated by many social and political factors, in this way distorting the results. Mayor and Swartz conclude that "None of the agencies (accrediting for schools or professional organizations) has succeeded in basing its accreditation on the quality of its graduates, rather than largely on qualitative standards." (1965:220)

Measurability

Some have taken the position that "anything that exists, exists in some amount," with the implication that it can therefore be measured. Two objections can be raised regarding this. Peter Drucker has called attention to the first, saying that

> the problem is rather that the important and relevant outside events are often qualitative and not capable of quantification. They are not yet "facts." For a fact, after all, is an event which someone has defined, has classified, and above all, has endowed with relevance. To be able to quantify one has to have a concept first. One first has to abstract from the infinite welter of phenomena a specific aspect which one can name and finally count. (1966:16)

Much of what is important in the ministry is qualitative and cannot be directly quantified. The second objection relates to the first. If certain qualities are to be measured, indirect indices must be used. While it is obvious that a certain person has empathy as a counsellor, there would appear to be no direct way to measure the quantity of empathy he has. The best that has been done to date has been to ask various people to judge how empathetic the subject is. Since many of the issues related to ministry are difficult to quantify, accreditation people generally retreat to things that can be counted, such as the number of books in the library, the level of endowment, or the number of academic degrees among the faculty. It is supposed that there is some relationship between them and ministry outcomes. On the face of it, often there seems to be little relationship.

Many of the qualities important in ministry are hard to quantify. Whether they can be enhanced by

theological education and tested is another question. Areas such as "spiritual formation" would appear to be of this nature, and yet they may be some of the most important features for ministry. We assume that there is some relationship between education and ministry, but to demonstrate it is not easy.

Diversity

Is an electrical engineer as-good-as a lawyer or a teacher? Most people would consider the question to be either illogical, foolish, or unanswerable. Yet this is precisely the question being asked of accreditation. For instance, Nicholls has observed that the "London B. D. is inadequate training for ministry in Nigeria and even in London." (Bowers 1980) That is to say the needs of ministry and the formation a person should have to minister in Nigeria are not the same as in London, and probably those of the present system are not adequate even for London. In any case, an equivalent formation in Nigeria is different from London. The same is true of ministry in almost any context. The problems of Bombay, India require understandings that are different from the rural Mayan communities of Central America. How then is "as-good-as" to be determined? The basis cannot be scholarship or even literacy. It can only be determined by the requirements of ministry in any particular situation, that is, to answer the question, what is the function of the ministry or what is it to achieve in that particular context?

Diversity may include many different aspects or areas. As Anderson observed, the lack of written materials in a particular language in no way indicates the abilities of the people to reflect theologically. (Kinsler 1983:158) In fact the usual measures may be counterproductive. Sales and Liphoko write "We saw that our reliance on measurement of academic excellence has blinded us to the kinds of excellence they were exemplifying." (Kinsler 1983:143) The only way diversity can be included and still maintain some credible sense in equivalence is if the goals of theological education are defined in each case, and there is some way to know if these objectives have been achieved.

Objectives

From where do we get our objectives? It would appear that in most cases they have been defined for institutions by either expatriates or nationals who have studied in the West and have copied from their experience. This has been done not only at the curricular level, but with respect to the content of courses, and in many cases the textbooks are translations from those the teachers used. The definition of ministry has come from the same sources.

If we examine the origin of the image of a minister or priest that is used today, we find that much of it came from the Middle Ages in Europe, with modifications from the Reformation and later. During the Reformation, the teaching ministry was set up as supreme, and the pulpit ministry was serious instruction. An example of this are Calvin's commentaries which were originally his sermons. Visitation, counseling, etc., were included, for the minister often was the only educated person in the community. Today in the West many of these roles have been taken by others— doctors, lawyers, psychologists—so the minister is more closely confined to a religious role, supposedly irrelevant to any social or political issues. Even the teaching role in the church to a large degree has moved from the sermon to the church school and other scheduled Bible studies for special groups.

With this loss of roles, Jenks and Riesman (1968: 201ff) have pointed out, ministers have pushed to become "professionals," which means that they are more accountable to their peers than to their "clients," in this case the congregation. The movement toward large congregations with more remote and formal relations between pastor and people would appear to contribute to this change, as does the development of large denominational bureaucracies. The level of accountability is greatly reduced, for the feedback cycle between action and consequence becomes very long and tenuous. As Sales and Liphoko have pointed out, "there is no reason except a financial one for a congregation to be so large that its members do not know or care intimately for one another." (Kinsler 1983:146) Thus the self-image of the minister has become strongly influenced by the "financial gain equals success" value of the non-Christian world view.

To adequately define the ministry and thus the objectives of theological education requires a much more rigorous formulation based on an understanding of the community and roles the minister should play. Some of the issues that should be considered for defining the role of the minister, as well as the kind of person who should take the role, and what he/she should know and be able to do, are the following:

1. Biblical definitions in the Gospels, Romans, I Corinthians, Ephesians, the Pastoral Epistles, etc.

2. Local leadership patterns, not only by whom and how they were exercised, but also how a person attains the role.

3. Roles of religious, spiritual, and healing ministries.

4. Where the present church practices came from, why, and how they have been modified by independent groups.

5. What prophetic roles need to be filled according to the existing community needs.

6. The present importance of formal education as perceived by the local and Christian communities.

The way education for ministry is conducted and the way it socializes the ministerial candidate are almost never considered in designing a program. Yet, as Saranson has pointed out, most learning occurs as "roles in settings." (1971:246) A clear example of the contrast in the socializing effect of the residence institution vs. extension was cited by Sales and Liphoko. Traditionally, putting two ministers in one church was like putting "two roosters under one henhouse roof. Whereas in previous cases the ministers had been trained individually and reproduced the conditions of their training, these ministers had been trained cooperatively and just as faithfully reproduced the conditions of their training." (Kinsler 1983:146) Creating a theological education program involves the design of a socialization process, intentional or unconsciously. Should it lead toward a life integrated in the community, or should it seek individual superiority and authority?

Accreditation

This brings us back to consider accreditation and its general purpose. Nevins, in his study of accreditation, writes, "The main effect of the accredited status for private secondary schools and for colleges seems to be prestige. It is a device for attracting students." (1959:313) The same message is transmitted to students. Adeolu Adegbola commented that education appeared to provide students with a "certificate of superiority," and therefore in some sense a license to exploit those without it. (1978:16) For places where education is difficult to obtain, theological education is seen as valuable, not for ministry, but as a stepping stone to further degrees, and a way to escape the hardships of rural life.

Selden, in his review of accreditation, stated that "The observation that the 'whole accrediting movement is a chapter in the struggle for the control of our higher institutions' is as true today as when George F. Zook, then president of the American Council of Education, uttered it twenty years ago."(1960:1) One of the purposes of control is to limit the market. Are we seeking quality education or prestige and control? It would appear that quality comes from people working together to "create a broad, uplifting, shared culture, a coherent framework within which charged-up people search for appropriate adaptations. Their ability to extract extraordinary contributions from very large numbers of people turns on the ability to create a sense of highly valued purpose."(Peters & Waterman 1982:51)

In the end, top quality education will come from people with a vision that inspires both teachers and students to dedicated service, to consecrate themselves to the purpose of doing God's will. These may be people without credentials, the official stamp of approval. They may have no prestige or pretensions, but they will provide an authentic simplicity and integrity to those around them of the image of Jesus Christ.

> You know that those who are supposed to rule over the Gentiles lord it over them, and their great men exercise authority (control) over them. But it shall not be so among you; but whoever would be great among you must be your servant, and whoever would be first among you must be slave of all. For the Son of Man also came not to be served, but to serve and to give his life as a ransom for many. (Mark 10:43-45)

> For consider your call, brethren, not many of you were wise according to worldly standards, not many were powerful, not many were of noble birth; but God chose what is foolish in the world to shame the wise, God chose what is weak in the world to shame the strong, God chose what is low and despised in the world, even things that are not, to bring to nothing things that are, so that no human being might boast in the presence of God. He is the source of your life in Christ Jesus, whom God made our wisdom, our righteousness and sanctification and redemption; therefore as it is written, "Let him who boasts, boast of the Lord." (I Cor. 1:26-31)

If equivalence is to be achieved in the midst of diversity, it can only be judged on the basis of its purpose. Which is better, a car or an airplane? It all depends on where one is going. The trip from New York to Santiago may be best taken by plane unless one desires to see the countryside on the way. Prestige and control have no place in the Christian Church and its educational work; achievement of God's will is all important.

BIBLIOGRAPHY

Abbot, Frank C. (ed)
1958 *Faculty-administration relations.* Washington, D. C.: American Council on Education

Adeolu Adegbola, E. A.
1978 *The future of education in Africa.* Ibadan: ACLCA

Bowers, Paul (ed)
1982 *Evangelical Theological Education Today: 1. An international perspective. 2. Agenda for renewal.* Nairobi: Evangel Publishing House

Drucker, Peter
1966 *The effective executive.* New York: Harper & Row

Hanson, John W.
1965 *Imagination and Hallucination in African Education.* East Lansing, MI: Michigan State Univ., Institute for International Studies, College of Education.

Jenks, Christopher & Riesman, David
1969 *The Academic Revolution* Garden City, NY: Doubleday

Kinsler, F. Ross
1981 *The Extension Movement in Theological Education: a call to the renewal of ministry* Pasadena, CA: William Carey Library
1983 *Ministry by the people.* Geneva, Switzerland: WCC Publications

Nevins, John F.
1959 *A study of the organization and operation of voluntary accrediting agencies.* Washington D. C.: U. S. Govt. Printing Office

Peters, Thomas J. & Waterman, Robert H., Jr.
1982 *In search of excellence: lessons from America's best-run companies.* New York: Harper & Row.

Sarason, Seymour B.
1971 *The culture of the school and the problem of change.* Boston: Allyn & Bacon, Inc.

Selden, William K.
1959 *Accreditation: a struggle over standards in higher education.* New York: Harper & Row

Selden, W. K. & Porter, H. V.
1977 *Accreditation: Its purposes and uses.* Washington, DC: Council on Postsecondary Accreditation

Part II: Tools for Reflection on Basic Issues in Theological Education

- ## Theological and Educational Foundations
  - **The Word of God, the Church, and the World**
  - **A Theoretical Framework for Theological Education**
  - **The Nature of Ministry**
  - **Basic Educational Issues**

- ## Spiritual Formation
  - **A Hermeneutical-Pedagogical Circle**
  - **Personal, Ecclesial, and Social Transformation**
  - **Three Fundamental Dimensions of Learning**
  - **Self-Development in Community**

- ## Structures, Ideology, and Values
  - **Ideology and Evaluation**
  - **Values and Evaluation**
  - **Para-Messages of Theological Education**
  - **Administration, Planning, and Finances**

- ## Contextualization and Globalization
  - **Contextualization**
  - **Globalization**
  - **Relationships with the Local Church and Community**
  - **The Local-Global Church**

The Word of God, the Church and the World

Down through history some programs of theological education have affirmed that their primary responsibility is to the Bible, the faith, the tradition, that they are called to prepare men and women to interpret and teach God's Word to the church and proclaim it to the world. Others have affirmed that their primary responsibility is to the church, that their task is to prepare pastoral agents to carry out the church's understanding of its mission and ministry. Still others have affirmed that theological education should give priority to the world and its needs, that its primary task is to equip the church to carry out God's will and pursue God's rule in the world.

The following diagram provides an idealized image of the relationship between these essential elements. God's Word, the church and the world are themselves interrelated, and theological education is related to all three. The latter is itself, at least potentially, a focus for all three, a point of convergence and interaction for all three, and possibly a critical point of tension with all three.

Theological students, teachers, administrators, church leaders, and members concerned about theological education need to examine and discuss these relationships. They may want to ask themselves whether their program of theological education has a particularly strong focus on one dimension, a weak focus on another, or a balanced concern for all three. They may want to consider whether their program's focus on the church enables the church to be faithful to God's Word and the world, whether its focus on God's Word provides an adequate foundation for understanding of and ministering to both the church and the world, whether its focus on the world provides new challenges and insight into God's Word and the church. They will certainly want to analyze and evaluate their curriculum's effectiveness in equipping students to integrate these three areas in their own lives, in their theology, and in their present and future ministries.

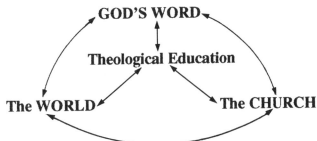

Step One

Participants may be invited to reflect on the diagram individually for five to 10 minutes and to write down their observations in light of the previous paragraphs and in relation to their program of theological education. If there are more than 12 people, they may then share their findings in groups of four to six.

Step Two

The groups may then be asked to focus on their program's strengths and weaknesses in relation to one of the three dimensions, with at least one group focusing on each. Each group may prepare a list of strengths, a list of weaknesses, and a list of recommendations regarding the curriculum and any other aspect of their program in relation to God's Word, the church, or the world.

Step Three

A plenary session may then receive the reports of the small groups, provide an opportunity for discussion, draw up a list of conclusions and/or recommendations, and decide on a process of further reflection, articulation, planning, and evaluation. This exercise may lead to a statement of the institution's or program's purpose, guidelines for the curriculum, and/or policies about student and faculty participation in church and community projects.

A Theoretical Framework for Theological Education

As followers of Jesus Christ we are called to "Seek first God's reign and God's justice" (Matthew 6:33). Some have been given specific gifts and responsibilities within the church, which is Christ's body; they are to use these gifts and responsibilities not simply to do the work of ministry but to equip and encourage others to participate in ministry; thus all the members will contribute to the building up of Christ's body in love (Ephesians 4:11-16). Theological education can and should play a critical role in this process, but we must be clear about the relationships between these essential elements. There is a danger that those who receive theological training may monopolize the gifts and responsibilities for ministry, either because they want to exercise leadership in that way or because the members want them to do so. Another danger is that the ministry may be so absorbed in serving the church that the church may neglect its calling to seek God's justice and peace for all people, and there are those who are so engaged in struggles for justice that they abandon the church or the church abandons them.

The following diagram is one simplified expression of how these relationships might work. It is intended to stimulate reflexion on the larger system of which theological education is a part. Any breakdown in the dynamic links between these elements may nullify whatever may be taught in the curriculum, so it is essential for all interested parties to examine their theoretical framework and the way it is actually working in their particular context.

God's Reign of Justice and Peace

Communities and Peoples

Congregations, Churches

Pastoral Agents

TEE

Pastoral Agents

Congregations, Churches

Communities and Peoples

God's Reign of Justice and Peace

Step One

Participants may wish to meet in small groups to study this diagram, to adjust it to suit their understanding of the role of theological education and its relationships to the other essential elements, and then to consider how well the system is working in their own particular contexts.

Step Two

After some 20 to 30 minutes' discussion in small groups the participants may present their findings in a plenary session. Further discussion will lead to greater clarification and consensus. Then they may wish to draw up a summary statement of their understanding of the theoretical framework for their program of theological education.

Step Three

The participants may wish then to consider the implications of this framework for:

- the recruiting of students
- the content of the curriculum
- the practical work of students
- faculty, facilitators, and mentors
- other aspects of their program

The Nature of Ministry

Ephesians 4:11-16 gives us a very important picture of the nature of ministry. V. 11 tells us that there are many kinds of ministries, i.e. services, within the church, the body of Christ. It mentions four or five kinds, depending on whether we read "pastors and teachers" as separate or as "pastor-teachers" at the end of the list. It seems evident that this list is not exhaustive; we could add other New Testament ministries or names, such as deacons, elders, bishops, and we might just as well add other terms for these and other ministries that have emerged down through history. The main point is that the church should recognize many ministries distributed among various people and not center all these responsibilities or gifts in one, the ordained pastor or priest.

Another important teaching is that those who may be identified as having a specific ministry, according to v. 11, are called to equip the saints, i.e. all the members, for the work of ministry, according to v. 12. The latter are the primary agents of ministry, the ministers, not the former. Even those whom we set aside for ordained ministry may be considered auxiliary ministers, whose task is to equip, enable, and mobilize the congregation for ministry.

A third essential lesson is that the work of ministry, vv. 12-13, includes all that contributes to the building up of the body of Christ, which clearly goes beyond what the ordained ministers and other specific ministries can possibly do. It requires the participation of all the members, which is why the vocations/the gifts/ the services must constantly be multiplied. The ministry is in fact the dynamic, mutual, self-development of communities of followers of Jesus Christ, in service to their neighbors, ultimately to the whole world.

In v. 14 we see what happens when this corporate understanding of the ministry breaks down, when some monopolize it and others are left out, when some, perhaps the vast majority, are not equipped and incorporated into the work of ministry. They remain immature and are easy prey to novel beliefs and deceptive schemes.

So it is clear in vv. 15-16 that we must all, every single member, in love with truth, grow up into Christ through the contribution of every member as essential parts of his body. The final phrases of this passage could hardly state more clearly, through so much repetition, that all of us are necessary to the whole.

Now we must ask ourselves several critical questions about theological education as we ourselves may have experienced it in the past, as our programs are now constituted, and as we would like it to be in the future. Some may feel that theological education has been misdirected, training only future clergy and training them to do the work of ministry instead of equipping others to do it. Others may feel that theological education has been counterproductive, excluding the natural leaders of the congregations and imposing as credentialed and paid leaders persons who have not earned recognition through service among their peers. Still others may point out that our patterns of professional training and professional ministry is an inevitable product of our modern social patterns.

The purpose of this exercise is to encourage church people (clergy and laity), theological educators, and students to examine the Ephesians model of ministry, to analyze their own practice and theology of ministry, and to explore the possibility of recreating today dynamic, genuinely shared ministry through alternative approaches to theological education. This challenge is posed through the following steps.

Step One

In preparation for this discussion, participants may be given copies of the above paragraphs and invited to make their own analysis of Ephesians and its workability today in their ecclesial and cultural context. The following questions may aid in this process:

- How can theological education open its doors to the whole church, i.e. to all who wish to participate in building up a mutual ministry, transcending the separation of clergy and laity?

- How can theological education demonstrate to the church that all members are ministers?
- How can theological education help to restore the dynamics of ministry, so that natural leaders emerge through their service?

Step Two

When they come together, participants may share their reflections, first in small groups and then in plenary. The group reports may be aided visually (newsprint, blackboard, overhead projector, etc.) in order to identify convergences and build consensus.

Step Three

Discussion should lead to plans or recommendations which may then be directed to those who can pursue them further. It may be feasible to propose a date for another meeting to evaluate progress and propose further steps.

Basic Educational Issues

There are many educational issues with respect to the whole theological education program. A few of these are indicated below in continua. Most programs will not be at the extremes, but somewhere along the line. It would be interesting for participants to rate their program on these different issues. Each person could make his/her own judgment, and then the group could discuss their different perceptions, for there will undoubtedly be differences. It will be especially interesting to compare the perspectives of students and tutors, staff and directors.

Following this, it would be valuable to brain storm the possible ways the program could be made more appropriate to the church and community. Then participants may want to produce a report with the most valuable and important suggestions for implementation.

Issues of Social Structure

These issues often reflect the status quo, and they may not be the desirable relationships for the body of believers.

1. Where are decisions made? Who has the power and authority?

Concentrated   Dispersed

Hierarchical   Democratic

2. What characterizes the relationships between tutor and students, administrators and staff?

Stratified   Equality

3. Are costs high, requiring external funds, or low, within the students' reach?

High   Low

Issues of Curriculum

1. Is the curriculum atomized, smorgasbord, or an integrated set of studies?

Atomized   Integrated

2. Is it open for many choices by students, few choices, or closed, allowing no choice?

Closed   Open

3. Are the studies related primarily to life and ministry or to the academic specializations?

Academic   Life related

37

4. Are the studies appropriate for the ministry/service the graduates will be exercising or only marginally so?

|_____|_____|_____|_____|_____|_____|_____|_____|_____|_____|_____|_____|_____|_____|_____|_____|_____|_____|_____|

Unrelated   Related

Concept of Communication

1. Are students passive receivers of approved information or stimulated to think through issues creatively?

|_____|_____|_____|_____|_____|_____|_____|_____|_____|_____|_____|_____|_____|_____|_____|_____|_____|_____|_____|

Passive   Active

2. Is communication one way, teacher to student, or two way, dialogic, interactive in discussion and reflection?

|_____|_____|_____|_____|_____|_____|_____|_____|_____|_____|_____|_____|_____|_____|_____|_____|_____|_____|_____|

One way   Two way

3. Does the essential apprehension of the material depend mainly on memory or on analysis and problem solving?

|_____|_____|_____|_____|_____|_____|_____|_____|_____|_____|_____|_____|_____|_____|_____|_____|_____|_____|_____|

Memory   Problem-Solving

4. Is study oriented for the student to be dependent on the input of others following graduation, or to develop independent study abilities and habits?

|_____|_____|_____|_____|_____|_____|_____|_____|_____|_____|_____|_____|_____|_____|_____|_____|_____|_____|_____|

Dependent   Independent

A Hermeneutical-Pedagogical Circle

In the past theological education tended to give priority first to academic, intellectual formation in terms of the biblical and theological content of the faith, later to the practical application of the faith to ministry, and only peripherally to the social, cultural, and historical context. In recent years it has become increasingly clear that these basic ingredients should be kept in focus throughout the entire process of formation, that the interrelation or tension between them is what makes them meaningful for the participants, and that the ongoing circulation between the three can become the driving motor throughout the curriculum and future ministry. The tendency is of course for all of us—faculty, students, and church leaders—to view the world, the faith, and the practice of ministry from our own perspective, which may well be one of privilege. Therefore we are challenged to view our local and global context from the perspective of the poor and marginalized, to reread the Bible from that perspective, and to pursue models of ministry also from that perspective. For many this approach has created or confirmed a fundamental epistemological break-through, and it has provided an essential critical tool for our theological-vocational journey. It is particularly relevant for TEE programs, because the students realize their studies in the context of the real world and the ongoing practice of ministry.

In the past the field of philosophy provided the intellectual frameworks, concepts, and perspectives that shaped people's understanding of reality and affected the other dimensions as well. Later the field of psychology played a similar role, and it continues to contribute important insights into human behavior, pastoral practice, and even the reading of the Bible. More recently the social sciences have begun to play a decisive role in our understanding of the social, economic, and political dimensions of reality, of the biblical story, and of pastoral practice. In each case new insight into reality raises new questions for the church's life and mission, for its reading of the Scriptures, for its understanding of the Gospel. Today many church people and theologians are saying that the overwhelming fact of our time is that the unjust distribution of power, wealth, knowledge, and technology is causing deepening poverty, hunger, and incalculable suffering for a growing majority of the world's population, killing 50-100,000 people a day, and that this fact should be a primary focus for our analysis of reality, rereading of the Bible, and pastoral practice.

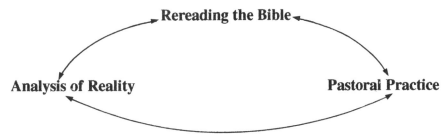

Step One

Participants may be asked to reflect individually and silently on their own spiritual-vocational-theological journeys in order to identify the critical experiences and influences that have led them to their current understanding of the world (reality), the faith (the Bible), and ministry. They may wish to jot down some notes on a blank sheet of paper. After some 10 minutes they may meet in small groups to share these reflections, identify common elements, and relate them to the work of theological education. They will want to ask themselves how their program can more effectively stimulate and accompany these critical experiences by focusing more directly upon the basic elements of the hermeneutical-pedagogical circle and the relationships between them.

Step Two

The small groups may share their findings in a plenary session. Discussion of these reports should lead to clarification of the diagram and the relationships between the three basic elements. The participants may then consider how the curriculum as a whole and the various courses individually might more effectively incorporate the hermeneutical-pedagogical circle.

Step Three

A commission may be named to write up recommendations, guidelines, and/or objectives for the future design of the curriculum and the preparation of courses. They may also wish to propose new learning experiences, new types of courses, and/or new resources to facilitate this process, i.e. the circulation between analysis of reality, rereading the Bible, and ministerial or pastoral practice.

Personal, Ecclesial, and Social Transformation

Education can be defined as a process of change. Theological education is concerned with the process of personal, ecclesial, and social change in accordance with God's purpose for humankind. Thus it is important to consider how our programs prepare our students as agents of personal, ecclesial, and social transformation. Insofar as TEE programs enroll leaders throughout the church, representing all sectors of the church, they are well suited to respond to this challenge.

Some theological and religious traditions place great emphasis on personal salvation to the neglect of the church and social change. Others focus primarily on the church, perhaps to the neglect of personal and social transformation. And still others are deeply committed to social action and service to the neglect of personal and ecclesial change. There is certainly room for different emphases and a great need for diverse ministries in these three directions. But a holistic understanding of God's purpose and God's reign must surely recognize not only the need for all three, but also the interconnection between them. The biblical writers would probably not even understand, much less accept, the individualism implicit in much of today's personal evangelism and pietism. They understood God's call in terms of a people (Israel) and a community (the church) for the sake of the world (the peoples—*ethne*). One of the fundamental challenges of theological education is to develop a clear and profound understanding of and commitment to integral human transformation as illustrated by the following diagram.

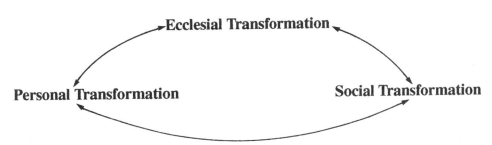

Step One

Participants may be asked to discuss, first in small groups, their understanding of the Gospel mandate for human transformation in these three dimensions. They may list biblical and theological bases as well as social, economic, psychological, and ideological understandings of sin and salvation under God's reign. They will want to examine the relationships and tensions between the three dimensions of the diagram.

Step Two

Participants may then, still in small groups, go on to consider how their current programs prepare their students for leadership in these three basic dimensions of human transformation. They will want to identify gaps and recommend changes as they look at the curriculum as a whole and at the individual courses. They may want to propose new learning experiences, new types of courses, and new resources.

Step Three

The groups may share their findings in a plenary session. Discussion may lead to a common statement that will summarize this understanding of theological education, list agreed upon recommendations, and propose steps for implementation.

Three Fundamental Dimensions of Learning

Educators have long emphasized that learning is not simply the accumulation of information, concepts, and knowledge. Equally important are abilities and attitudes. This is certainly true of theological education, which is formation for ministry. The following exercise may be used by theological educators, students and others as they plan and as they evaluate their programs. They may choose one or more of the options suggested.

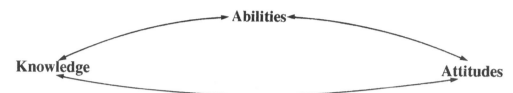

The cognitive dimension (knowledge) of theological education is vast, and it is complex, but it has received most of the attention of theological education and absorbed most of the time of theological students. By the time they finish their studies, these students are expected to know an awful lot about the Bible, theology, the history of the church, and the various aspects of ministry. Perhaps the greatest need here is to develop more effective strategies for building effective learning sequences that lead to holistic understanding.

The affective dimension (attitudes) is far less understood and far less developed but no less important. It has to do with the nurture of feelings, values, and commitments that correspond with the biblical, theological, and pastoral knowledge that theological education has been so concerned about. Surely no ministry can be very effective without humility, compassion, solidarity, without a spirit of reconciliation, peace, and deep conviction, without genuine faith, hope, and love. These attitudes are not easily formed in classrooms. But TEE students may find themselves daily in situations where they can indeed be nurtured—at home, at work, in their communities, and in their congregations. TEE educators need to dedicate their creative resources to the development of this dimension.

The skills or abilities that the different ministries require are likewise essential. Theological education programs have most often focused on the communication of the Gospel through preaching, teaching, and evangelization. Some have added skills for worship, which might include music, liturgy, drama, and even art. Others are now giving attention to community organizing, popular education, cross-cultural communication, and inter-faith dialogue. Any of these skills can become a top priority for the church's life and mission in a given situation.

Option One

Participants may wish to consider essential elements for a core curriculum that all students need, whatever their present and future ministries. They may wish to divide up in groups to work out a list of general objectives in the traditional areas of Bible, Systematic Theology, Church History, and Ministry or choose other areas. Each group should list their objectives under these headings: "knowledge," "abilities," and "attitudes." They should also consider the relationship between these three types of objectives. The groups will then report to a plenary, which may decide how to strengthen or revise the curriculum to achieve these objectives.

Option Two

Participants may wish to focus on particular ministries such as pastors, evangelists, Christian educators, social change agents, professionals in society, etc. Individuals or small groups may then list their objectives under the three headings of the diagram and consider the relations between the different types of objectives. As they report on their work, all will gain new insights from each other.

Option Three

The participants may choose to work on specific courses, that is, to evaluate existing materials or design new ones. They will want to spell out specific objectives under the three headings and consider the relations between them. They will then present their work for consideration by their colleagues in plenary session.

Self-Development in Community

The TEE movement has increasingly affirmed that real learning is a process of self-development with appropriate resources and accompaniment. TEE students are by and large mature leaders in their local churches and communities. They bring to the process of theological education a wealth of experiences, concerns, questions, and goals. Our programs should therefore build on their past experiences, respond to their present realities, and help them move toward their future ministries in the church and in society. We should pay particular attention to the process through which they enter the program and encourage them to build their own curricula according to their interests and needs, making use of diverse resources and methods of learning that best suit their situation.

The following diagram suggests that theological education may be understood essentially as a process of self-development with appropriate resources and accompaniment. It is very difficult, on the one hand, for people who are active church leaders, heads of families, and fully employed in secular jobs or in the home to take on and maintain a demanding academic program. It is evident, on the other hand, that such people bring from their daily life an excellent context for meaningful and effective theological-ministerial formation. The challenge to theological educators is to assist and enable that difficult but promising process, i.e. to find and prepare necessary tools and to be available on a regular basis for personal, theological, and vocational accompaniment together with other peers.

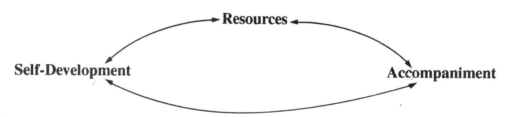

Step One

Participants may review the process of admission in their program in order to see whether in fact it challenges each student to take responsibility for his or her own formation for ministry. They may wish to ask the following questions and, if necessary, to design worksheets for the students to fill out.

- What have been your past experiences in ministry, and what are your priorities for future ministry?
- What formal and non-formal preparation for ministry have you received in the past, and what are your priorities for further preparation?

Step Two

Most extension students are very busy with the daily routine of family, work, church, and social responsibilities. They need appropriate resources and close accompaniment in order to maintain a steady rhythm of study in the midst of all these responsibilities. The following questions may help to identify additional and more appropriate resources and means of accompaniment.

- What course materials and other resources can be made available for the students' regular study process?
- What are the best means of personal accompaniment on regular and occasional bases?

Step Three

Many extension programs use a very limited range of study materials, but others are multiplying the possibilities through diverse methods or modes of learning. Every set of study texts or modules is limited, but these new approaches are open-ended and practically unlimited. Any program can encourage its students to explore their particular areas of interest through reading courses, research courses, action/reflection projects, experiences in ministry, social involvement projects, etc. All they need is guidelines as to the process of design, approval, accompaniment, reporting, and evaluation of these modes of study.

- What open-ended modalities of learning are available through your program? What might be developed?
- What guidelines or guide-books are available for these modalities? What should be prepared?

Ideology and Evaluation

There are different and opposite opinions about the function and scope of ideology. (Apple 1979, 20) But it is commonly accepted that ideology permeates and influences the ways in which we think about things and the ways we do things. Usually it is taken for granted; it becomes part of our "common sense." Ideology exerts a strong influence in the way we process our values and carry out our actions so that we experience it as "built into our living, into our sense of reality." (See Kennedy, 1985, 331-344; Bonilla 1986,25-51; Schipani, 1985) Nothing in society is immune to ideology. Certainly not education.

The relationship between ideology and education has been amply discussed. Education has been clearly recognized as one of the "apparatuses" through which a particular ideology is transmitted and maintained. Education has the "persuasive" function of influencing and controlling consent. Whether or not education has been replaced by mass electronic media as the primary "non-coercive" ideological apparatus in our present society (Kennedy 1985, 343), it continues to be the main "apparatus" for the church in maintaining and conveying its self-understanding of both its nature and mission in the world. The following observations are intended to provoke discussion among the various interested parties of theological education.

First, ideology, understood as a particular view of the world in light of a particular set of ideas, is not only inevitable but it is necessary. In order to make sense out of the world wherein we live, we need those "ideas" to frame it. Therefore, we can say, nobody escapes the "ideological game," not even the church. As William Kennedy puts it, "ideology permeates all social existence." (1985, 333)

Second, these sets of ideas represent the understandings of a particular social group in society, by which the people act and function. On the one hand, this denotes the action-oriented function of ideology, since it allows a particular group or community to work in society for the benefit of the group. (Bonilla, 1986, 27) On the other hand, it reveals the existence of different ideologies in a society, which struggle for some quota of power in that society. This second aspect relates to what Michael Apple calls one of the distinctive features of ideology, that is, the power-conflict link. (Apple, 1979, 21) Can we honestly argue that this seeking or holding power is a dynamic absent both in our ecclesiastical denominations and our theological institutions?

Third, these sets of ideas can be as systematic and elaborated as the ideological platform of a political party or as unorganized and simple as the common sense of public opinion. What is important is that these ideas dominate—consciously, as in the first case, or unconsciously, as in the second—the thinking and action of a group. (Apple, 1979, Chap. 1; Grundy 1987, 106-114)

Fourth, as ideology represents the vision of a particular group, all ideologies reveal and hide part of reality. Our knowledge of reality is always a partial interpretation of reality. There is not a "revealed ideology"—within or outside the church—that would encompass a perfect knowledge of our world. (Bonilla 1986, 29) Therefore, because of the partiality of knowledge and the interests they represent, all ideologies should be subject to analysis and criticism.

Fifth, ideology assumes an "hegemonic" character when a particular set of ideas, representing values, interests, and assumptions of a particular group in society, is presented as "the universal, rational, and natural way" to understand and act in our world. Some "negotiation" with other existent ideologies may take place, but only in order to keep the primacy and survival of the hegemonic ideology. (Kennedy, 237) Here ideology works for the maintenance and justification of a particular political and economic system, or, in the case of theological education, of a given set of doctrinal statements and practices. When this happens, it becomes political and theological dogmatism.

Sixth, ideology may assume a "utopian" character if it "envisage(s) a qualitative transformation of the (present) conditions of human life." (Baum 1975,236) But this requires "clarity about the nature and function of a dominant ideology. . . . " (Kennedy, 237) Thus, through the understanding of the hegemonic ideology and within it, it is possible to find elements that will lead to resistance to and transformation of that hegemonic ideology and of the reality it justifies and maintains. (Giroux 1983)

Seventh, the ideology most difficult "to recognize and to unmask is the ideology of one's own community." (Kennedy, 236) To use a biblical image, it is easier to find "the speck" in the other person's eye than to see the log in our own eyes." We are not aware of the "eyeglasses" through which we see our world. That is why it is so important to exercise self-criticism of our own beliefs, values, and practices in theological education. Otherwise we will remain under "ideological captivity." (Bonilla 1986, 36)

Eighth, it is necessary to distinguish between "ideological mediations" of our faith and "ideologization" of our faith. We express our faith by using, borrowing, adapting, adopting, and inheriting "images" from our historical context. Those mediations which enable us to interpret and live out our faith are "inevitable and necessary." But when the theological assumptions and practices misrepresent the real conditions of society, pervert the message of the Scripture, and even refuse any criticism—whether from the Scriptures or from society—we can talk of ideologization of the faith. (Bonilla 1986, 34)

Ninth, not all ideologies are equally valid "in making sense of the world." The lesser the distortion of reality—and of the Scriptures—the greater the validity of an ideology. The greater the representation of the interests of the majorities of a society, the greater the validity of an ideology. (Bonilla 1986, 50)

Tenth, formal education has generally transmitted and helped to maintain the ideology of the dominant groups of a given society. Those groups are usually the most economically and politically powerful groups in the society. In the case of theological education it is also true that a particular theology, that is, a particular vision of the church, is transmitted. And that vision corresponds to the understanding of those who run and control the programs, or of the churches which support the programs, or both.

Eleventh, it is extensively accepted that ideology both affects the curriculum of formal education and is reflected in it. What is taught and how it is taught reflect the values and interests of the dominant ideology. The content of the curriculum, the methods used to communicate it, the patterns of relationships between teachers and students, the ways and reasons for evaluation, all this is not neutral. They are "embedded" in a particular vision of the world, society, and persons. (Apple 1979) In the case of theological education, because a dichotomy is usually made between theology and education, we may find different levels and kinds of congruence between the what and the how of the curriculum, but both will reflect the influence of the dominant ideology of a given society.

Twelfth, ideology is reflected not only in the overt curriculum, but more subtly in the "hidden" and "null" curriculums. The hidden curriculum is shaped by the academic, interpersonal, and institutional routines of the teachers and students in the program, e.g. promotion of academic competitiveness, expectations of the relationship between teachers and students and of those with the institution, schedules, and organizational structure. (Schipani 1985, 29) The impact of such aspects in the students' worldview cannot be underestimated. Null curriculum is made up of "the contents" that are not taught in a particular program, the teaching methods that are not used, the criteria of analysis that are not promoted. In other words, everything that is neglected or disregarded, consciously or unconsciously, in the design of the curriculum of a theological program, reveals the influence of ideology in and through the educational program. (Bonilla 1986, 45-47)

Step One

Copies of the above paragraphs may be distributed in anticipation of the workshop or meeting at which they will be discussed. Participants may be requested to underline their copies and also to note in the margins examples of each of the 12 points.

Step Two

Participants may meet first in small groups to share their reflections on and examples of the points raised in this paper. Then they may be asked to list the basic elements of the dominant ideology of their society, of their church(es), and of their program of theological education. They may wish to draw up three parallel lists under these three headings in order to demonstrate the similarities and differences.

Step Three

The small groups may present their findings, preferably with visual aids, in plenary. Participants will want to clarify, compare and perhaps consolidate these reports. Finally, they will want to make recommendations for further evaluation and planning of the future ideological position of their program.

BIBLIOGRAPHY

Apple, Michael

1979 *Ideology and Curriculum,* Boston, Mass.: Routledge and Kegan Paul

Baum, Gregory

1975 *Religion and Alienation: A theological reading of sociology,* New York: Paulist Press

Bonilla, Plutarco

1986 Ideología y Currículo: equilibrio y tensión, in *Pastoralia* 17 (Dec.) 25-51.

Giroux, Henry

1983 *Theory and Resistance in Education: A Pedagogy for the Opposition.* Massachusetts: Bergin & Garvey Publ.

Grundy, Shirley

1987 *Curriculum: Product or Praxis*, London: The Falmer Press.

Kennedy, William B.

1985 Ideology and Education: A fresh approach for religious education. In *Religious Education*, 80 (Summer) 331-334.

Schipani, Daniel

1985 Pautas epistemológicas en la bùsqueda de alternativas para la educación teológica. Paper presented in Buenas Aires: ASIT. Argentina.

Values and Evaluation

To evaluate, one must have values. In some sense, these are ideals for action against which reality is to be judged. Thus there are two aspects to values, the idea/thought/word and the action. When we impute values to something, we are reversing the process, deducing the value from the action that produced it. There is therefore a rationale, a reasoning process that leads either from the stated value to the action, justifying it, or from the action to the value, declaring why the action was carried out.

Evaluation then is the process of comparing the actual situation with the ideal, and making a judgment as to whether the actual state corresponds to the ideal, or to what degree it corresponds. One of the perennial problems is that the value on which the judgement may be based is unexamined, accepted by faith, and blind faith at that. As the value tends to be an ideal state, something desired, the action usually does not measure up. If the departure from the ideal is great, it can cause frustration, or reinvigorated efforts to achieve the ideal. On the other hand, if the action appears to contradict the stated value, we tend to consider it to be hypocritical.

Many values that are "understood" in a community are cultural, passed on by the community, and are not overtly recognized by those who live by these values. For instance, an important North American value is comfort. Automobiles are designed for maximum comfort; homes are also built this way. When a North American is in a situation that is not comfortable, too hot, too cold, unpleasant surroundings, the person tends to be upset, out of sorts. Yet this value is never articulated; it is unconscious for most people. The experience of one youth worker in Latin America reveals similar problems. For a number of years during youth conferences, he held sessions relating to dating, courtship, and marriage. At one point the young people were asked to list the characteristics they thought important in a spouse. Being a Christian group they consistently affirmed, as expected, that the person should be a Christian. In second place the predominant response was that the partner should be light skinned. Yet, they all would have denied being "racist." Many of the values of any group of people are unconscious.

As mentioned above, values provide the rationale for action. Behind each value there is a reasoning process, usually unconscious, that is used to justify the action. On the surface the action may appear justified, yet examining the rationale might lead one to realize that the people involved do not in fact approve of the premises. For instance, a person who has been in a certain ministry for many years may justify the ministry as serving a particular group of needs. However, the truth may be that the need has ceased to exist, but the need for a job has not. Thus, the rationale for the position is in fact to provide employment for the person, a reasoning that would be rejected categorically by the incumbent. Many institutions today and their personnel are in fact in this position. However, to examine the situation would be too threatening, so the organization continues its existence, unself-critically.

Values are more than mere preferences, sentiments, or feelings. Some philosophers have taken the position that ethics is fundamentally aesthetics, that is, moral judgments are nothing more than feelings. Feelings change and are truly subjective. Values, on the other hand, are social, public. A value is usually shared by others of the community and in any case it is recognized by both outsiders and insiders as a value. Outsiders may not be committed to it, but they recognize it. An example would be the North American emphasis on saving time, which is strong among many people. As one friend from India asked one day, "What do Americans do with all the time they save?" Of course the answer is, they don't know. But it shows that though Americans hold the value that time is important, and most are committed to it, people from other communities may recognize it as a value, though they may not be committed to it.

As seen in the previous paragraph, commitment is another aspect of values. Commitment also has degrees, ranging from very weak to total. The degree of commitment becomes obvious in Christian circles as we observe the different style of life of different persons. For instance, for some, attendance at church once a week may be considered enough, along with making a nominal contribution. For

49

others, being a Christian involves time for meditation and prayer; it means ordering life to attend services, to check that one is being honest and fair in business activities, with family, etc. The whole life is viewed as under the control of Christian values.

With respect to TEE we can observe the same. Some of those involved have viewed TEE as a prime way to spread the Gospel and to help believers mature into leadership positions for the edification of the body of believers. Others have held positions in institutions that operate TEE programs; if they do not accept work in the TEE program they have no job. These people may have a commitment only as far as TEE provides a job; when it no longer does, they abandon any pretext of commitment.

In education this problem of values is always with us. It is said that we will teach as we have been taught. Are there better ways? Should teaching be done differently? Does an authoritarian mode by the teacher lead to authoritarianism in those being taught? Jesus taught that this is a worldly attitude. Should it be changed? (Mk. 10:42-43) There is very little that we do that is value free.

As Christians we recognize that there are many values inherent in the faith, ones to which believers should be committed. These values may conflict with the community/culture where we have been socialized. We need to recognize that in no case do the two sets of values fully correspond, Christian values and cultural values, and also there is no cultural group that does not hold some values that are congruent with the Gospel. Thus all cultural values are in some sense under the judgment of God and may need to change. One of our problems is to distinguish between those values that are critical for the Gospel and those that are fundamentally indifferent. Some would consider hair length and style or amount and type of clothing as critical. Others would consider these values as indifferent. Each person and Christian group must struggle with these values and come to their own conclusions, while allowing some latitude to those who disagree.

Exercise One

Take students and faculty to visit a church service of a denomination or sect that is quite different from their own. Following the visit, gather to discuss the experience. Have each person write down those points where they felt at odds with or uncomfortable with what went on in the service. Collect these on a flip chart or blackboard and reflect on each one. Why did they feel uncomfortable or feel what went on was wrong? What reasons would they give to justify their actions? Are there Biblical reasons that they could use to substantiate their position? Could they live with these differences?

Exercise Two

Gather a group together who have had experiences with people of various nationalities or of various language/ethnic groups. What were the differences that they noted among these different people as they associated with them, especially those characteristics that annoyed them. Again list these and examine the list to determine as well as possible why these aspects annoyed or disturbed them. Then reflect on whether that was a conflict with one's own cultural group, or whether it was really something that was in conflict with the Gospel. What conclusions do they reach?

Exercise Three

Students and faculty should then reflect on the values expressed in the TEE program. Are there values of cooperation or independence and competition? Does the program offer ways for the learners to build community and express concern for each other, or does each person tend to be isolated and go his/her own way? What relative values do men/women/young people/elders have? What relative value is placed on experience/academics? What relative value is given to different ethnic groups in the local society?

Para-Messages of Theological Education

A school cannot be more democratic than the society in which it exists.

—**Anonymous**

The art of educating people is in all nations so closely tied to the form of government that it is not possible to effect a considerable change in public education without doing this in the States' own constitution.

—**Helvetius,** *Discourse IV*

The quality of learning . . . in an organization is affected by the kind of organization it is.

An organization tends to serve as a role model for those it influences.

In hierarchically structured organizations there is less motivation for self-improvement, and there are more blocks to learning (like anxiety) than in more democratic organizations.

—**M. Knowles,** *The Adult Learner*

Education is never neutral. Particular theologies, ideologies, philosophies and political stances always underlie a training program of any kind. Particular views of reality, general value systems, are always implicit, if not explicit. The tendency is for the intended philosophy or theology to be relatively explicit in the overt curriculum, but less so in the "hidden curriculum," which embraces the various other aspects of any training program: administration, relationships, buildings, time-tabling, types of faculty and students, and so on. All these aspects carry their own message, the "para-message," which may be quite powerful and which may or may not comply with the official philosophy of the college or program in question. Obviously, the overall context of a training course also carries a strong para-message.

Following are some examples of para-messages conveyed through the structures, style, and ethos of theological institutions.

1. A program which accepts only young men conveys a strong message that only youth (not older people) and males (not females) should be seriously considered for Christian training and ministry.

2. An institution with a high percentage of missionary faculty conveys the idea that few local people are qualified to teach at this level. It may convey the idea that overseas personnel are somehow superior, particularly if missionary staff are housed and paid better than local staff.

3. The ways faculty treat students and students treat employees convey powerful messages about the way pastors and other leaders should treat ordinary church members.

Faculty, students, administrators, graduates, and others concerned about theological education need to examine not only what are the declared, intended purposes and contents of their program, but also its para-messages, which may be hidden and unintended, which may even by contrary to the intended purposes. In each case the para-messages may be very different from the examples mentioned in this exercise. The following questions are provided as a way to launch a discussion of this issue which in turn may lead to further analysis and action.

1. Do you agree with the first quotation above? If so, what are the implications for your theological education program? If not, do you want your program to be more democratic than your society? In what ways is this achieved or could it be achieved?

To what extent is "democracy" a Christian value and to what extent is it merely a Western value? Does democracy relate, for example, to the Reformation principle of the priesthood of all believers? To the diversity of gifts? To the sinfulness of all, the image of God in all, and the love of God in Christ for all? Does democracy appear in non-Western forms which might be more applicable to your part of the world than in its Western versions?

2. Do you agree with the second quotation above? If so, what implications does this have for students coming into your theological education program from the public education system of your country? What kinds of para-messages are carried by your public education system? How far are these compatible with the philosophy and worldview of your theological education program?

If it is hard to change public education without government constitutional change, how much more freedom do theological educators have to change their education and to convey a different message?

3. Do you agree with the Knowles quotations above? If so, what are the implications for your theological education program?

How would you describe the organization which runs your theological education program? Hierarchical or democratic? Rigid or flexible? Geared more to the needs of students, teachers, or church authorities, etc.? What human relationships prevail?

There may be various administrative and governing levels, e.g. the immediate administration, the university or college to which it may be related, the church or ecumenical group which it serves, and perhaps an outside examining or accrediting body to which it is accountable. Think carefully about your own philosophy and worldview as communicated directly and overtly in the program. Consider the philosophy and worldview of each sector which controls the program. Each at some point contributes to the para-message or hidden curriculum, subtly or not-so-subtly conveyed to students. Do these various para-messages fit together comfortably with the overt philosophy or are the students exposed to various mutually contradictory influences and messages? Which messages "speak" loudest—values and approaches to life taught in the study materials and seminars or those conveyed by the various administrative structures in which the program operates? Is there anything that should be changed? How might this be done?

Administration, Planning, and Finances

In some cases TEE programs are administered directly by theological colleges or seminaries, in other cases in conjunction with these institutions, and in other cases yet by churches or by ecumenical bodies. The way the programs are administered has a direct bearing on how decisions are made for these programs, how programs are planned, and how they are financed. These in turn have their impact on the effectiveness of the programs among those for whom they are designed and administered and on the efficiency with which they are conducted.

The operational principle of TEE is that students should be trained in context, as they are immersed in the business of daily life. Ideally, the body responsible for the recruitment of students should be the local church rather than the educational institution. The needs of the local church and of the community in which it witnesses should influence the shape of the TEE program. It follows that the local church and/or community, the students, graduates, tutors/facilitators, etc. should have a deciding input into how the TEE program is administered, how it functions, how it is financed, and eventually how it is evaluated. In this way, the beneficiaries of the program come to recognize the program as theirs as well.

In cases where the TEE programs are administered by educational institutions or in conjunction with them, every care should be taken to ensure that students and local interests are truly (not tokenly) represented in the administration and planning. Similarly, with church-run TEE programs, local pastors, students, lay and community representatives should be involved with denominational and program administrators in the operation of TEE.

It cannot be over-emphasized that the integrity, effectiveness, and efficiency of TEE programs demand that the lines of responsibility and communication between all parties involved in TEE be clear and unambiguous. These should run in both directions: from bottom to top and from one side to the other. Mutuality in sharing and in service should be the prevailing spirit, not the desire to control and dominate.

Whatever its means, the local church should be encouraged to help with the financing of TEE. Students should contribute to their education by bearing a percentage of its costs. While TEE in Third World countries cannot in the foreseeable future dispense with funding from external sources, programs must seek to avoid either control by or over-dependence on those partner-agencies that are sources of funding for national TEE programs.

TEE should aim at long-term economic stability by prudent planning and economic self-reliance by weaning itself from external support and efficiently monitoring its cost-effectiveness. This long-term project of stability, self-sufficiency, and cost-effectiveness should be the concern of all those who have a stake in the programs—students, graduates, tutors/facilitators, the local church, the local community, pastors, TEE program coordinators, church administrators and partner-agencies.

Following are suggestions for the evaluation of administration, planning, and financing of TEE programs. As indicated above, all interested parties should ideally participate in this process.

Step One: Descriptive

1. Administration: Set out the program's administrative structure, showing lines of authority and responsibility. Indicate the lines of communication between the central office and regional centres, between tutors and students, between church administration and TEE program.

2. Planning: Describe how plans are made for the achievement of the short-term and long-term goals of the TEE program. List the individuals and groups who participate in planning at every stage.

3. Finances: Indicate who are involved in budgeting for the entire program. Show what financial load is carried by the students, by the local church, by the denomination(s), and by external partner-agencies. Describe how records are kept, how fees are collected from students, and how funds are dis-

bursed by the TEE administration.

Step Two: Evaluative

1. Illustrate the administrative structure of the TEE program by placing a one directional arrow (→) or a two directional arrow (← →) between the following pairs.

Regional Center	—————————————	Local Center
TEE Administration	—————————————	Students
Church Administration	—————————————	TEE
Tutors	—————————————	Students

2. On a scale of 0 (no involvement) to 10 (full involvement) rate the participation of the following in planning for TEE.

Church Administrators	_____	Local Community Representatives	_____
TEE Administrators	_____	Tutors/Facilitators	_____
Students	_____	Local TEE Centre Coordinator	_____
TEE Graduates	_____	External Partner-agencies	_____

3. Fill in the percentages in the following as best you can:

External contributions to TEE budget	_____
Denominational contribution	_____
Local Church contribution	_____
Students contribution	_____
Others (specify)	_____
Total =	100%

4. Answer the following questions:

Is the external contribution to the TEE budget higher or lower than in previous years? _____

Are there plans to reduce the dependence on external funding in near future? ____ Eventually? ____

If the answer to the previous question is <u>yes</u>:

Who will bear the costs now met by the external partner-agencies?

The denomination	_____	Students	_____
The ecumenical body	_____	A combination of the above	_____
The local church	_____		

Are plans being made to build up resources to meet TEE needs if and when missionary personnel leave? ____ If so, what are these plans?

Step Three: Recommendations

Having analyzed the response to Steps One and Two above, what recommendations would you (the evaluators) make to planners and policy makers for the efficient and effective administration, planning, and financing of the program?

What suggestions would you make for the implementation of your recommendations and for the evaluation of the implementation process?

Contextualization

Inherent in much ministerial education is a lack of social analysis. That . . . is reflected in the life of the church where there is a woeful ignorance of the nature of contemporary society, and therefore there is also a lack of perception of the real nature of powerlessness. Without such social analysis . . . Christians cannot be expected to begin to tackle creatively the forces leading to exploitation. Consequently, the church cannot realize its task of being an agent in God's liberating and redeeming action. . . .

Within many theological colleges there is a strong emphasis given to the Scriptures and systematic theology. Yet these are seldom related to social analysis. Indeed this lack of a holistic approach within training communicates itself via ministers to the churches, where few Christians see life in its wholeness.

Report of Workshop IV
Consultation on Ministerial Formation
Reported in *Ministerial Formation* 45, 1989 (p. 20)

There is always a context for any form of education, and it is vital that Christian training relate creatively and redemptively to that context. The context has various components and various levels which must all be considered if a program is to be thoroughly suited to its environment and speak to its needs, hopes, and challenges. The following questionnaire may be used as a basis for constructing a tool suited to the evaluation of contextualization in particular programs of ministerial formation.

1. How far does your training program respond to each of the following contextual levels? Which are given greatest emphasis? Are you happy with the balance of your program's response to these different levels?

- the context of the local supporting church(es)
- the context of the local community

- the context of the regional synod, diocese, or presbytery
- the context of the geographical region

- the context of the national denominational structure
- the context of the whole church in the nation (ecumenical context)
- the context of the state or province and of the nation.

- the continental or regional ecumenical context (e.g. Africa, Pacific)
- the overall continental or regional context

- the worldwide ecumenical context
- the global context

At the wider levels of contextualization, one moves into the concept of globalization in theological education.

2. In what specific ways does your training program respond to each contextual level?

3. We may also approach the question of context in terms of its different aspects or its (inter-related) components. "Context" is often narrowly defined in terms of cultural traits, perhaps from the standpoint of functional anthropological presuppositions or in terms of religious worldview. These are essential components of any context, but there is much more.

In its attempts to contextualize theological education, which of the following aspects does your training program take into serious account? What other aspects of the context are important in your situation?

- the geographical and climatic context
- the historical context
- the traditional cultural and multi-cultural context
- the changing contemporary context (usually a mixture of old and new)
- the socio-economic context
- the religious inter-faith context
- the political context (local and global)
- the ecclesial and theological context
- the educational context
- other aspects of context:_____

How, specifically, do you address each aspect in your program? Are you happy with the above approach? Are there aspects of the context you should more directly address?

4. We need to apply principles of contextualization not solely to the content of what we teach, but to the other components of our program as well. Consider the following questions:

- How do you contextualize the context of your curriculum? Faculty, students and others may wish to discuss specific forms of contextualization in the choice of subjects and in the syllabus for each. How do you contextualize church history, ethics, evangelism and mission, Christian education, theology, biblical studies, etc.?

- How do you contextualize the methods of teaching and learning? Do you take account of traditional means of teaching practical skills, passing on knowledge, values, stories, songs, etc.? Would some of these methods of teaching and learning be more appropriate than a heavy reliance on lecturing?

- How do you take account of the kind of education students have experienced in the local school system? This is not always well contextualized itself, nor genuinely indigenous. Many school systems reproduce older colonial styles of education, now replaced in the Western countries which first exported them. So it is not always wise for theological educators to adopt methods used in local schools, especially if these represent a lot of rote memorization and highly formalized classroom procedures which create a gulf between teachers and students. If students have not learned to question and to think for themselves, this should be encouraged. We may not wish to reproduce poor education systems, but we do need to take account of them when their graduates come to our TEE programs.

In general, TEE seminars are not devoted to lecturing but to discussion and to other creative means of teaching and learning, so this should help us move away from unproductive to more productive means of contextualizing methodology.

- How do you contextualize the structure and administration of the TEE program? This can raise a variety of questions about financial arrangements, venues and times of meeting, administrative procedures, etc. It is important to remember that administrative structures always carry their own "hidden" message.

Generally speaking, an adequately contextualized TEE curriculum should reflect clearly the particular situation, problems, needs, and perceptions of the society and church where it is based. Since the program may be taught in various centers over a relatively wide area, it may require guidelines in the tutors' handbooks to help them contextualize more specifically in their own regions. The overall curriculum and methodology should be in many ways different in Africa, Asia, or Latin America than it is in the West. And it should be different in diverse parts of a continent. Even where international accreditation standards are being pursued, there should still be ample room for a strong local flavor in each TEE curriculum.

Adequate contextualization also demands real student immersion in church and society in various forms of learning and of creative ministry and service. Faculty, students, and others may like to reflect on how far the program takes advantage of the unique opportunity TEE offers for such involvement in real life and ministry in the local community. (Seminaries must often create somewhat artificial "field work" situations. TEE students should naturally be involved in real ministry assignments.) The challenge may come not so much in getting them involved in meaningful church work, but in encouraging and helping them to integrate what they learn in home study and seminars with what they learn on the job and in life. There is also a challenge to become involved, even in a small way, in new forms of ministry they have not tried before. Learning is limited if students work only in their immediate church settings and never in the wider community. It is also limited when they try only one kind of ministry—e.g. Sunday School teaching, preaching, or youth work—for many years.

5. What steps does the program take to help students integrate practical and theoretical learning? This is more than merely "applying" what is learned in home study and seminars; it also involves reflection on what is learned in everyday life and ministry.

6. What opportunities do the students have to become involved in community work, not only church work? The two often overlap, of course, but adequate contextualization is unlikely if students' practical ministry is confined to church people and to programs directed inwards toward the church alone.

7. Every culture and society, like every human being, is marred by sin. Hence total contextualization would mean at some points infidelity to the Gospel and the Christian way of life. At what points in curriculum, administrative structures, and methodology does the program deliberately resist contextualization? Why? Are there other points where present contextualization needs to be questioned? How do you train your students to develop, where appropriate, a genuine prophetic stance? Contextualization also needs to be balanced and extended by globalization if it is to avoid becoming another form of parochialism.

Globalization

The following questionnaire may be used for discussion of the degree to which the TEE program has attained a good measure of "globalization." Questions should be added or omitted as appropriate. For further ideas and practical suggestions see the WCC book which is based on a conference held at Bossey, Switzerland, on this theme, viz, *The Teaching of Ecumenics*, edited by Samuel Amirtham and Adriaan Geense, 1987. The following questionnaire is based on an earlier one designed by H.•M. Mills from suggestions by denominational staff executives for the June 1980 Biennium of the Association of Theological Schools in Denver.

Historically, Christians have been the one part of the world's people who have been most "globally" minded. One thinks of the different parts of the world. The Coptic Church in Ethiopia and the Mar Thoma Church of India have these traditions. The early Nestorians reached as far as Japan and China. Xavier and the early Jesuits reached the Far East. The Russian Orthodox Church established missions in Alaska and along the Northwest Coast of North America. The Moravians went to America to work with the Native Americans and among the slaves of the Caribbean. William Carey had his world map on the wall of his shop so he could pray for people around the world. David Livingstone had a map on the wall above the loom on which he worked, and he prayed for Africa. The modern missionary movement has taken Christians to more places and peoples, frequently earlier than the most adventuresome businessmen.

A "World Christian" is one who plays an active role in the ministry of the church to the whole world. Obviously, most cannot go to other countries and cultural communities, but all can and need to have the vision of bringing the Gospel to the entire "inhabited world," the "oikoumene." With this vision, the "World Christian" will participate in this worldwide outreach at least through prayer, encouragement, giving, and reaching those within his/her area who need the Gospel and its lifegiving power.

1. Does your TEE program have an explicit policy of helping students to become "World Christians" in the fullest sense of the term? If so, how is the desired outcome defined in this regard and what are the specific goals of the program? In practice, do you think these goals are being achieved?

Because TEE courses do not extract students from their own communities and because these communities are often small rural towns and villages, there may be a greater danger than in metropolitan seminaries that students remain rather parochial in outlook. Contextualization is generally easier and globalization more difficult in such settings.

- What specific strategies are in place to ensure adequate globalization in your TEE program? How is each core subject affected by this concern?
- If your program has an explicit policy of globalization, is this policy affirmed and practiced by all faculty, or does it tend to remain the project or "hobby" of a few?

2. To what extent do teachers and students use the work of theologians, commentators, and other writers from various parts of the world (including the Two-Thirds World) in day-to-day studies?
- Is there a place in your curriculum for some use of the arts of other peoples of the world?

3. Do you have any faculty and/or visiting teachers from other parts of the world? It is recognized that TEE programs are unlikely to have foreign students. It is also recognized that in nations where there has been strong missionary dominance in the past it is now considered vital to localize faculty. For purposes of globalization, however, it should be noted that an all-local faculty is not necessarily the ideal. Since TEE courses are often attached to a residential college, a healthy international mix of faculty and students in that college can contribute to international awareness in the extension arm of the school.

4. If your program is run by a single denomination or congregation, what steps are taken to ensure that students have regular opportunities to hear the views of other Christians as expressed by repre-

sentatives of these other traditions themselves? What provision is made to obtain visiting teachers from other churches? Have students frequent opportunities to mix with Christians and with theological students, in particular, from different denominations?

5. If your program operates in a multi-faith, multi-ethnic and/or multi-lingual environment, how far does it reflect this reality and utilize it as a resource for teaching and learning?

6. How far does your library reflect an international and ecumenical view of the world? Do book collections and journal subscriptions support such a view?

7. What factors in your curriculum and overall training program encourage parochialism (as opposed to contextualization)? What factors encourage a global perspective in terms of such categories as mission; justice issues; understanding and appreciation of the varieties of peoples and cultures; grasp of important international events, trends, and needs; knowledge and appreciation of the worldwide church in its various forms; issues of human need, war and peace, the environment, and so on?

8. What practical involvement do students have in the spiritual and practical needs of their community? How are they taught to extend their learning in local situations to a deeper understanding of similar needs in other parts of the world and of appropriate and inappropriate means of ministering in such situations?

9. How is globalization furthered in the teaching of particular subjects? Examples:

- CHURCH HISTORY—Is this taught with adequate consideration of the churches in the Two-Thirds World as a whole? Is mission history integrated with church history, and is church history in turn integrated with general history? From whose perspectives is history taught?

- ETHICS—Does this course embrace social as well as personal ethics? Does it connect local concerns, where appropriate, to global systems and institutions? Does it provide students with sound theological and practical guidelines for citizenship of their own nation and of the world?

- THEOLOGY AND BIBLICAL STUDIES—Do students use the insights of a variety of theologians, commentators, speakers, and others—women as well as men, poor as well as rich, lay as well as clergy, representing a number of countries and cultures?

Relationships with the Local Church and Community

The major value of TEE is its commitment to training in context, to the selection of students by the local church, and to a basic understanding of service to a specific community in which the church is set, of which the church is a part, and to which the church is called to serve. TEE generally operates on the principle that the responsibility for recruiting students and for participating in their formation lies with the local church. Educational programs should aim at meeting the needs of the local church as that church in turn seeks to minister to the needs of the larger community. It follows that the TEE program should be related to the local church and to the local community context. The question is *How?* The answer is that, ideally, the relationship should be a two-way, reciprocal one between the TEE program on the one hand and the local church and community on the other.

Students and tutors/facilitators should be expected to participate in the life and worship of the local church and, as part of that church, in service to the larger community. This involvement should be a required part of the TEE course.

The local church should be expected to provide information about TEE to prospective students, supply facilities for seminar meetings, provide opportunities for students to participate in the life, worship, and service of the church, support the work of students, and assist with the supervision of students and the evaluation of their work.

If it is accepted that the relationship between the TEE program and the local church/community should be *reciprocal*, and if that mutuality in sharing is understood and accepted in terms of the expectations of students/facilitators and local church/community spelled out above, it should be possible to test the quality of that relationship at any given time. The aim of such testing should be to improve the quality of the relationship. An evaluation process, which if possible should involve the pastors, lay persons, community leaders, tutors/facilitators, students, graduates of TEE programs, etc., may use the following steps:

Step One: Descriptive

1. Set out briefly what the students and tutors/facilitators have done or are doing in the life of the local church and the local community (e.g., planning and/or conducting worship, preaching, leading in Bible study or in youth fellowship, supporting a drive for environmental reform, etc.).

2. Set out briefly the ways in which the church and/or community have supported the students and tutors/facilitators (e.g. providing opportunities for student/facilitator participation in worship, supervising of students, providing of facilities for seminars, etc.).

Step Two: Evaluative

1. Grade the quality of student participation in each aspect of the local church.

	Less than Adequate	Barely Adequate	Adequate	More than Adequate
Congregational life	_____	_____	_____	_____
Worship	_____	_____	_____	_____
Service outreach	_____	_____	_____	_____

2. Now grade the tutors'/facilitators' participation in these areas.

	Less than Adequate	Barely Adequate	Adequate	More than Adequate
Congregational life	____	____	____	____
Worship	____	____	____	____
Service outreach	____	____	____	____

3. Now grade the church's/community's provision to the students and tutors.

	Less than Adequate	Barely Adequate	Adequate	More than Adequate
Information	____	____	____	____
Facilities for seminars	____	____	____	____
Opportunities to participate in worship	____	____	____	____
Support and encouragement	____	____	____	____
Supervision	____	____	____	____

Step Three: Recommendations

The results of these questionnaires should be tabulated, compared, and discussed. They may reveal differences of perception between students, facilitators, pastors, and others. Participants may want to analyze why some areas are barely adequate or less than adequate, and they should suggest concrete ways for improvement. It may be important to initiate some changes immediately and to set dates for others.

The Local-Global Church

The Church of Jesus Christ is local, regional, national, and worldwide. It is independent and denominational, evangelical and ecumenical. It is Asian, African, European, Latin American, North American, Caribbean, Middle Eastern, Pacific, etc. It is rich and poor. It has innumerable racial and cultural expressions. It carries on in its memory, its theology, its patterns of organization, its worship, and its programs many ancient and recent heritages with diverse rationales that have grown out of particular experiences, struggles, controversies, problems, and needs.

Theological education itself is an expression of these realities, and it can be one of the most important resources for the church in its struggle to be faithful. On the one hand theological education, especially TEE, is concerned with the preparation of local leaders and congregations for ministry in their particular contexts. On the other hand it opens up to local leaders and congregations the history and current realities of the global church. Both dimensions are essential. A church which is only concerned for its local expression can become parochial, blind to its own limitations, and ignorant of the critical learnings and creative resources of the wider church. A church which focuses too much on the universal and historical can fail to express its faith in appropriate, relevant ways for the people it serves. So one of the major challenges of theological education programs is to equip leaders and congregations for faithful, local expressions of the global church.

One of the greatest failures of the church down through history has been its disunity. Jesus prayed that his followers would be one (John 17). Paul stated again and again that there is only one church and one Spirit (Ephesians 4, 1 Corinthians 12, etc.). Insofar as the church is the body of Christ, it must seek to be united above and beyond and through all its diversity. So too theological education must help the church to discover and deepen and express its unity, locally and globally. We must of course recognize that many theological institutions have in the past been created as or later become bulwarks for particular ecclesiastical, theological, and pietistic traditions, equipping their students to hold and defend these positions against other competing positions, perhaps for very understandable reasons. Nevertheless they must all, sooner or later, face up to Christ's mandate, Paul's teachings, and the one Spirit's leading for unity.

Following are three exercises that can be used by theological educators, students, and church representatives as they deal with these issues. They may wish to adapt these exercises or create new ones for their own process of evaluation and planning.

Exercise One

Beginning in small groups and continuing in plenary, the participants may discuss ways in which their theological education program is so involved in local needs and realities that it fails to draw on the long history and vast resources of the wider church that might help them to respond more faithfully and more effectively to these needs and realities. They might eventually draw up in one column a list of their own limitations in this regard and in a parallel column a list of recommendations for broadening and deepening their formation for ministry by drawing on the church worldwide. It will be important to review these lists after 3, 6, and/or 12 months.

Exercise Two

Using the same process, beginning in small groups and continuing in plenary, the participants may wish to consider to what extent and in what ways their program fails to relate to the local context, circumstances, problems, and needs. They might draw up a list of inadequacies in this regard and add beside it a list of recommendations to overcome these inadequacies. They will then want to review these lists at a future date to evaluate their progress and make additional recommendations.

Exercise Three

Working in two groups, the participants may be challenged to consider how their theological education program contributes to the unity and disunity of the church. One group may work out and present a list of those factors in the curriculum and in the whole life of the institution that contribute to unity. The other group may work out and present a list of those factors that contribute to disunity. After full discussion of these lists, they may wish to make a third list of recommendations in order to work toward greater unity. Here again they should plan to review their findings and recommendations after a specified period of time for evaluation and further planning.

Part III: Tools for Evaluation and Planning of TEE Programs

- Curriculum
  - Curriculum Design
  - Basic Commitments throughout the Curriculum
  - Objectives and Outcomes
  - Adult Education Perspectives

- Study Materials, Experiential Learning, and Seminars
  - Writing Style for TEE Materials
  - Standards for TEE Self-Study Materials
  - Experiential Learning
  - TEE Seminars

- Students
  - Accessibility of TEE Programs
  - Assignments and Assessment
  - Obstacles, Delays, and Dropouts
  - Graduates: Source of Evaluation

- Facilitators
  - Faculty Selection and Development
  - Facilitator Roles and Student Roles
  - Student Evaluation of Courses and Facilitators
  - Education for Self-Development

Curriculum Design

Theological educators often design their curricula without the use of a model, though they may look at samples of other theological curricula. A better new or revised curriculum can generally be obtained by using some of the comprehensive work which has been done on curriculum by professional educators.

The following discussion questions are intended to help faculty and students evaluate their TEE curriculum and the process by which it was arrived at.

1. When the TEE curriculum was first designed, what attention was given to **curriculum design models** worked out by professional educators? Were any resource people with professional training in curriculum or in education generally consulted? What attention was given to literature on curriculum design processes?

If such resources were not used, on what was the curriculum based? Was a coherent philosophy/theology spelled out for the process or did the curriculum grow out of a rough combination of what the teachers had studied in their own training, what other local programs offer, and what needs were felt to be most important among the intended participants?

2. Most curriculum design models start with some kind of **situation analysis** or at least an analysis of the needs of the constituency and prospective students. Has an adequate situation analysis been undertaken as the basis for the TEE program, or is it based mainly on accreditation requirements or on an existing residential school curriculum?

How often has an analysis of the situation and the intended participants been up-dated? A review every few years would be useful in most programs. What mechanisms are in place for implementing changes in curriculum in response to changing needs?

What kinds of considerations were looked at in your situation analysis? Needs of churches in your constituency? Needs and problems in the society (regional and national)? Total context of the TEE program? Need for developing a global perspective? Gifts and ministries to be developed in connection with projected numbers and types of church workers likely to be needed over the next 10 years? Burning educational issues for our world today?

3. If local and regional **needs of churches, students, and society** were analyzed, how were the needs determined?

- by asking social scientists and reading their books?
- by teachers in the program?
- by a survey of clergy and laity, including potential students?
- by a survey of community needs through interviewing local people and talking with government and service agencies?
- others?

All these may well have valuable input, but we should never forget to ask potential students what their felt needs are. Nor should we forget to survey church people and the general public if our program is to meet perceived needs and not merely the needs we believe they have. The different insights of those involved at various levels are all important. Their needs must be met if they are to "own" the program.

4. Most curriculum design models also recommend deriving **clear objectives** from the situation analysis. Can members of the faculty clearly state the general objectives of the TEE program without having to consult a prospectus to remind them? In other words, are these goals both clearly spelled out and well-known to all faculty, who draw upon them naturally in their day-to-day work?

Are these objectives spelled out officially in terms of what the student is expected to achieve rather than in terms of what the syllabus is supposed to cover? Are the students' achievements at the end of the course measurable in terms of the stated objectives?

What studies have been done of graduates of the TEE program to indicate how well they have attained the goals of the program and how effective they are in life and ministry? Are the results of these studies satisfactory? If not, how might the curriculum be altered to help the program better attain its goals? If such a study has never been undertaken, would one be useful or necessary? How often should such studies be carried out? They need not be costly and could be relatively informal, but they will probably require feedback from the graduates at least every five years to maintain a curriculum which meets current needs and achieves most of its goals.

To what extent are the overall goals of the TEE program taken consciously into account in the design of each subject in the curriculum? Can each subject be clearly justified in terms of those goals?

5. Discuss the extent to which the TEE curriculum caters for whichever of the following **considerations** are believed to be important:

- Careful account taken of individual needs, gifts and calling. This calls for numerous "open" elements in the curriculum, such as independent, directed studies, study contracts, wide choice of electives and of assignment topics within courses, etc.
- Account taken of the different "domains" of learning—cognitive, affective, skills, and some would add spiritual growth.
- Emphasis on lifelong learning and on learning how to learn for oneself.
- Emphasis on development of critical thinking, problem solving skills, "conscientization."
- A good balance between reflection and action, theory and practice, theology and life.
- Strong emphasis on both contextualization and globalization.
- Emphasis on integration of all strands of learning, including life and practical ministry.
- Care to avoid the loss of integrity; care to ensure that subjects do not become such a smorgasbord of choices that there is no integrative theological whole in the student's life and mind when s/he graduates.
- Concern to set theological education in the wider framework of a good general education, as far as local conditions permit. This may be done by requiring an appropriate educational level for entrance or by including some general education courses, which might be done through another school, in the overall curriculum. A good teacher can also provide many general insights in the course of more specialized teaching. Wherever possible, it is desirable that faculty have an educational background broader than just theological training.
- Emphasis on the wider mission and holistic growth of the church (more than a curriculum simply geared to maintenance of the status quo in church and society).
- Provision of adequate tools for Christian social analysis.
- Cognizance of work done by psychologists such as Fowler and Kohlberg on faith and moral development stages. (One need not agree with all aspects of the theory of such writers to find their work helpful, even in cross-cultural contexts.)
- Recognition that no curriculum can be neutral and that the belief system behind the curriculum should be spelled out, with attention given also to the "hidden" curriculum inherent in administrative structures, etc.
- Awareness that there are many ways to plan a curriculum, other than through traditional subject areas. Thematic curricula, spiral curricula, and mixtures of these with traditional curricula are well-suited to some needs.
- Full provision in all aspects of the curriculum for spiritual formation. This implies a philosophy of how this is achieved. Is this done through compulsory chapel sessions twice a day or twice a week? Through legislated devotional times? Or what?
- Remember that the curriculum also includes the environment in which a person studies, interacts with other students, faculty, church people, how seminars are conducted, etc., not just the "courses" studied.

Basic Commitments throughout the Curriculum

Theological institutions usually try to cover vast areas of biblical, theological, historical, and pastoral studies. At the same time each program should be very clear about the essential foci and/or perspectives that it wishes to develop among the students and their churches in their particular context. One of the most important things that directors, teachers, students, board members, and church representatives can do is to clarify these central foci or perspectives and then to consider how these foci or perspectives are or should be present in all parts of the curriculum and perhaps throughout the life of the institution or program.

Some institutions will want to ensure that their students receive a theological formation that is both truly evangelical and truly ecumenical. Others will want to be sure that women's perspectives are present in every course and every activity. Others will insist that their diverse racial, ethnic, and/or cultural heritages are appropriately represented in their personnel, study materials, ethos, and lifestyle. This goes far beyond offering a course on ecumenism or women's concerns or pluralism. It requires a basic commitment throughout the curriculum, the administration, and the life of the institution.

Faculty, students, administrators, and/or church representatives may work on this concern in several ways. We shall suggest just three options here. This can be an occasional or regular dimension of evaluation and planning, as interested groups review periodically their priorities and ask themselves whether they are progressing in the application of these priorities.

Option One

Participants may be asked to identify three or four essential foci or perspectives that should permeate their curriculum. They may be asked to think about this individually before the meeting or at the outset, then share in small groups, and finally discuss their findings and develop a consensus in plenary. Then they may lay out a chart with these foci or perspectives along one dimension and the various academic departments or even specific courses along the other dimension. Then they may divide into teams to fill in the corresponding boxes, i.e. to indicate how they are now developing these foci or perspectives in each academic area or how they plan in future to do so, as the following sample suggests (much more space would be needed).

	Women's Studies	Justice-Peace	Nature-Ecology
Biblical Studies			
Theological Studies			
Historical Studies			
Ministry Studies			

Option Two

Participants may choose to deal with fundamental conceptual and methodological concerns as they plan and evaluate their curriculum. They may, for example, want to make a concerted effort to overcome the dualism between the spiritual and material dimensions of life, so prevalent in many cultures and church traditions. They may wish to ensure that theory and practice, reflection and action are held together throughout the curriculum. They may want to include audio-visual, artistic, musical, and popular media in every course that they offer. One way to bring about greater cooperation in developing these emphases is to offer a workshop exercise in which the participants review past efforts and explore new possibilities. The following chart suggests one way this exercise can be done (each group should identify its own priorities).

	Spiritual-Material	Theory-Practice	Alternative Media
Biblical Studies			
Theological Studies			
Historical Studies			
Ministry Studies			

Option Three

An altogether different approach to curriculum evaluation and planning is to identify the central concerns and foci of the local culture. The participants may be asked to identify these central concerns or foci and then consider to what extent they are present in their current courses. They may wish to make a chart, as we have done above, and then they may go on to consider the possibility of restructuring the entire curriculum around these themes. The following sample is based on the creative experimentation of a theological training program in Africa.

	Nature	Health	Spirits	Family	Community
Biblical Studies					
Theological Studies					
Historical Studies					
Ministry Studies					

Objectives and Outcomes

One of the most useful and significant approaches to curriculum development and course design has been:

- Define your objectives.
- Select the means (resources, methods, sequences) to reach these objectives.
- Compare your results to your objectives.
- Redesign the means.

These steps can of course be repeated any number of times until the outcomes match the objectives satisfactorily. This concept can be useful to students as well as educators, for ideally students should participate in the development of the curriculum and in the design of their courses by defining their objectives, choosing the means to reach those objectives, and evaluating their achievement of those objectives.

In order for this cycle of planning and evaluation to work, however, we need to define our objectives in terms of observable and measurable behavior. Course designers, teachers, students, and evaluators need to clarify exactly what the students must be able to do at the end of each course and at the end of the curriculum, so that all can see that the objectives have been achieved. Thus both planning the learning process and evaluating the results can be clear and fair and exact.

Some educators and students rebel at this approach because it seems to be mechanical and dehumanizing. We do not all learn the same ways or in the same sequences. There should be more spontaneous and creative approaches and routes to learning. This concern can be met by including more open objectives that reflect and encourage all dimensions of learning, especially the imagination, feelings, commitments, and values.

At the same time it is necessary for educators and students to set down as clearly as possible their objectives and the ways in which they will evaluate the learning that takes place. This is not to place teachers in judgment over students or students in judgment over teachers—though both kinds of evaluation are very common. Rather our common purpose should be to enable us all to prepare for ministry. In that sense the objectives should be closely related to the knowledge, skills, and attitudes that are necessary for effective ministry.

Instead of grading students by some arbitrary standard, some educators have suggested that grades should reflect personal progress, i.e. comparing their knowledge, skills, and attitudes at the beginning and end of a course or program. This can be done by giving a pre-test as well as a final exam. Both should cover the same areas, though for obvious reasons the questions should vary. The results will then show not only how well each student measures up to an arbitrary standard but also how much s/he has increased her/his knowledge, skills, and attitudes.

Following are three exercises that can be used by theological educators and students in order to define their objectives and evaluate their outcomes in an ongoing planning process. One of the most important results of this process may be that students will develop greater motivation for learning and continue using these basic planning tools in their future ministries. The same basic approach can of course be used by local congregations and other church organizations for their own planning and evaluation.

Exercise One

Theological educators and/or students may wish to plan and evaluate their work in specific courses by listing in parallel columns their objectives, the resources-methods-projects-sequences they will use to meet their objectives, and the ways in which they will measure achievement of their objectives. For balance and comprehensiveness they may list objectives dealing not only with knowledge but also with abilities and attitudes. They may work out these plans individually or in small groups (each planning one course), then discuss them in plenary session.

Exercise Two

Another approach is for the participants to work through the same process by academic area. Teams of teachers and/or students may develop parallel lists of objectives, resources-methods-projects-sequences, and evaluation guidelines for the Bible, theology, history, and ministry (or other) departments.

Exercise Three

The third suggestion is to work through these same procedures for interdisciplinary courses or seminars that will enable advanced students to test their readiness for the multiple tasks of ministry, which are themselves interdisciplinary. This will help to identify strengths and weaknesses in earlier course work as well. In all three exercises the participants should plan to review their work after a given period of time.

Adult Education Perspectives

Theological Education by Extension has expanded access to theological studies to include adults of almost all ages. Much typical classroom teaching and learning has taken pedagogical (literally, for children) principles as the basis for curriculum. Those working with adults should consider the differences that they bring to the process. Here are some of the characteristics of adult learners that need to be incorporated if learning is to be effective.

1. **Motivation**. Adults tend to pursue studies from some personal desire, to reach some personal goal, rather than from a socially imposed routine. Consequently their motivation is internal, not imposed, and tends to be higher.

2. **Experience**. Adults' experience is broader and tends to be more unique for each individual. They want to base their learning on their experience and to use it as a source.

3. **Autonomy**. Adults have achieved a degree of independence and expect to be involved in setting goals and in the process of selecting how to reach those goals. They are self-directed.

4. **Transitions**. Adults frequently choose to study because of some life change and want to learn how to cope with these changes. They may experience anxiety from not having studied for many years, or at all in formal educational settings. These changes may be related to conversion, rededication, or second careers.

5. **Utility.** Adults see time as important, as they see years pass. They want to learn what will be useful now, not for some future career.

6. **Classification.** Adults, due to having used language longer, often have more fixed categories and stereotypes. At the same time they may be aware of ambiguities from their experience. This paradox may be an obstacle to certain types of learning.

7. **Teaching.** They want an environment of respect and trust where they can express themselves and not be seen as subordinates of the teacher or facilitator.

The question is, are we treating adults as adults, or as large children? We should examine our materials and procedures in TEE (and in institutional theological education as well, since all of these students have left adolescence) in order to adjust them to the characteristics of the people involved. To do this we might take one of the lessons or courses we typically use and review it with respect to the above criteria.

The faculty and students could meet to examine the material, write individual critiques, and then enter a joint discussion of the material. Following this, individuals or teams could be selected to reedit the material to take into consideration the responses, and then the whole group could gather to review the results. The following questions may help to guide the writers and test their work.

1. Do the learners have any choice with respect to what they will study, how they will carry it out, and what they will be expected to know or do?

2. Do any of the activities to be carried out involve their own experience and knowledge? Will they relate the information/activities to their daily life?

3. Why are they studying this subject? Does it relate to their ministry/life, or is it just to fulfill requirements for a diploma?

4. Are they learning to learn, or are they merely expected to absorb material for later response?

5. What experiences of the learners are called into play by this course/lesson?

Writing Style for TEE Materials

Many course designers in TEE do not give much thought to the vital matter of readability—the matching of the material to the reading level of the students. Yet we know a student may easily become frustrated when asked to study books which are even two grade levels above or below his/her own reading level. Readability can make the difference between success and failure in TEE since so much depends on reading and since many of our programs operate in non-book cultures.

In many countries educators have worked out tests for grading students' reading levels and for measuring the difficulty of the reading material. Those writing for TEE would do well to consult reading specialists and local teachers' training colleges or university departments of education for assistance in this area. This is important at all academic levels—reading is a skill which continues to develop and which is not learned once and for all in the early school grades. Rudolf Flesch many years ago devised a useful readability formula for determining the difficulty of written material in terms of U. S. grade levels (which must be adjusted in countries where students are studying in a second language). He also has a formula for measuring human interest level in written materials. (See his *How to Write, Speak and Think More Effectively.* Signet Book, New American Library, 1963.) Other such formulas exist as well.

Another method of determining readability is to set comprehension tests on sample passages taken from different parts of the study guides, textbooks, etc. Since few theological writers consider readability very seriously, and since textbooks and TEE materials tend to vary in their difficulty level in different sections, it is wise to test samples from several parts of each book.

Where material is too difficult, it is necessary to alter it, pick another textbook, or provide the student with substantial help in the form of vocabulary insets, explanations, outlines, and so on. While we should be able to alter our own TEE materials to suit students needs, it is often more difficult to find alternative textbooks, especially in languages which have few theological books. It is mainly in these latter cases that plenty of help must be provided, both in the TEE materials which accompany the difficult textbook and in the seminars.

Experience shows that reading materials are more likely to be too difficult than too easy, and that many theological teachers never realize how little their students actually read of required texts or how little they understand! This is especially true in a second or third language. On the other hand it should never be assumed that students can understand everything easily, simply because the material is in their own language! (How many native English-speaking students have great difficulty with theological texts?) Ideally, every theological college and extension program would have at least one faculty member who could (perhaps among other things) act as a consultant and teacher of language and reading—even in the higher level schools. Advanced students too often need help with advanced reading and language skills which can greatly enhance their learning. It is also vital that all faculty work together to help develop language and reading skills. *"Every teacher is a teacher of reading,"* consciously or not!

What follows is a list of accepted principles of good style, applied to TEE. These come from various sources, including William Strunk's classic, *Elementary Principles of Composition.* From this one can, with appropriate additions and alterations for local needs, develop a working checklist to assist TEE course designers.

CHECKLIST ON WRITING STYLE

1. Write at a level appropriate to the student group. Cultivate a simple style, but don't talk "down" to people. Even marginally literate adults are not children and must never be treated as if they were.

2. Avoid a style which is pedantic, moralistic, or heavily didactic. "Talk with" the students; don't "lecture at" them.

3. Make your text "user friendly." Write in a natural, conversational way as much as possible.

4. Never use a long or difficult word where a simpler one will do as well. Avoid unnecessary jargon. Theological and other specialized terms may be used as needed, but should always be explained and illustrated in a sentence when this aids comprehension.

5. Avoid long paragraphs. Vary sentence length, but have none too long.

6. Work with a plan and make the paragraph your basic unit of composition.

7. Use the active voice as much as possible.

8. Put statements in positive rather than negative forms as much as possible.

9. Omit needless words.

10. In summaries, keep to one tense.

11. In English at least, place emphatic words more towards the end of the sentence.

12. Keep related words together.

13. Avoid sweeping statements and over-generalizations. Avoid tame, colorless, hesitating, and non-committal language as far as possible.

14. Always quote accurately and give your source.

15. Write vividly. Build with nouns and verbs and use adjectives and adverbs sparingly. Let your writing communicate energy and vitality. Don't mix tenses without proper transitions from one to the next. Do not overwrite. Avoid rich, ornate, "purple" passages. Avoid too many qualifiers—words like *very, rather, somewhat,* but do use them when you wish to avoid overstatement. Use definite, specific, concrete language. Avoid a lot of abstract nouns and abstract language (unless you are writing for a highly sophisticated group).

16. Always be clear. The writer knows what is meant; check that someone else does.

17. Don't try to cover too much material in one lesson or course.

18. Don't overstate. Avoid sticky-sweet, saccharine writing of the super-"spiritual" type. Write in a warm but not a "slushy" manner.

19. Use culturally meaningful humor where appropriate.

20. Use stories as often as you can, longer ones and short, illustrative anecdotes.

21. Build human interest. Write about people and events, and sometimes animals. Give people names, families, home towns, etc. rather than just saying "a man" or "a child" did such-and-such.

22. Write about believable characters, not perfect people and "goody-goodies."

23. Use plenty of words which have a natural gender, or are names, occupations, personal pronouns or terms referring to a group of people (crowd, folk, parents, cousins, etc.).

24. Express coordinate ideas in similar form, so the reader more readily sees the likeness of content and function (e.g., parallel constructions in the Beatitudes: "Blessed are . . . ; blessed are . . . , etc.).

25. Constantly test out your material with the students, revise and rewrite where necessary. Don't expect your work to be perfect all at once. This also means it is generally unwise to put a first draft of your TEE course—or perhaps any draft—into permanent form if it cannot easily be altered and improved. You may have a better looking course but will not be able to improve or update it easily or cheaply when necessary.

26. Use orthodox spelling. Do not try to spell in "smart" ways. This confuses the student.

27. Give as much explanation as necessary, but do not explain too much.

28. Use figures of speech with care. They are useful but should not be overdone. Don't mix metaphors.

29. Don't take shortcuts at the cost of clarity.

30. TEE lessons are meant to be interactive, so you should not write too much unbroken prose. There should be frequent opportunities for the student to respond in writing or in some other way, going over what has been taught or working through it in new applications.

31. Avoid any allusions, figures of speech, idioms, etc. which may not be understood by students. Take special care when writing for second language students.

32. Many writers like to include a small "box' with new vocabulary for the lesson at the beginning of that lesson. They also like to write a good paragraph or two as an "interest-catcher" to get students interested in the lesson at the outset.

33. Always use inclusive language. Even our writing style carries its own para-message.

34. Avoid any language, jokes or allusions which encourage stereotyping of people or discrimination on the basis of race, sex, ethnic background, etc.

35. Avoid language or allusions, comments, etc. which could offend any readers unnecessarily. If any group, viewpoint, religion, ideology, or person is criticized, this should only be done for good reason and after careful thought and consultation with others who must take responsibility with you for what appears in your courses.

Standards for TEE Self-Study Materials

The best way to establish a TEE program is usually for several churches or colleges to do this cooperatively. This is good ecumenics and also good economics! In such a situation, a number of different people may begin to produce TEE materials, and it becomes necessary to set up some kind of quality control. Minimum standards are generally set up, and those writers who wish their materials to be used by the program as a whole need to conform to those standards. This does not restrict churches or colleges in the use of their own materials among themselves, but it does protect the overall standards of the joint venture. Similar standards usually need to be drawn up for the conduct of TEE classes and for various administrative procedures. Associations in such countries as Brazil, Papua New Guinea, and the Philippines have set up their own standards for TEE self-study materials, and many others are doing the same in one way or another.

It will immediately be evident that procedures for setting minimum standards and procedures for self-evaluation are similar in many ways. Often the two can be done together in a workshop or seminar. One great advantage of setting clearly defined standards is that all course designers know what these standards are, and they can evaluate their own work to a large extent. This saves leaders from much of the onerous task of critiquing the work of their colleagues and explaining why a workbook its writer thinks is superb is, in fact, quite poor and entirely unsuitable for the TEE students! With good guidelines for writers, basic mistakes are avoided and corrected by the authors at the outset. Much time is saved, and much expense and unpleasantness are avoided.

Following are some general categories which may prove useful in setting minimum standards for self-study materials. They are also good categories for evaluation. Some of the categories are taken from an earlier, duplicated set of standards used by the Brazilian TEE association, AETTE (*Padrâo AETTE para Livros Autodidácticos*, 1977).

1. Content

- Theological acceptability to all participating institutions and churches.
- Avoidance of factual error.
- Nothing which could be interpreted as discriminatory against another group, stereotyping of people on the basis of race, sex, age, religion, etc.
- Suitable objectives and content for reaching those objectives in the light of the needs of the students and the overall purpose of the program.

2. Educational Value

- Material should be genuinely self-instructional.
- Educational methodology should be good, e.g. plenty of opportunity for student interaction with text; clear goals and learning routes which lead directly to these goals; material should move from known to unknown and explain all new concepts thoroughly.
- Ample encouragement for students to think for themselves, solve problems, develop their own perspectives—not mere repetition of memorized facts.
- If programmed instruction is used, material should be properly programmed; many courses are not. Also, there should be good reason for using this method rather than a workbook or other format.
- All sections of course should be well integrated.
- Application to real life needs should be evident.
- Right educational level for intended student group.

3. Assignments

- Set at right level for students.
- Practical as well as library assignments wherever possible; involvement in the community encouraged.
- For most students with little educational background, assignments based on reading and writing should be limited, with more attention to practical exercises.
- Variety in type of assignment; avoid heavy reliance on essays and exams.
- Progressive assessment rather than single exam at end of course.
- Assignments chosen to relate to main objectives of course and to fit the type of material being studied.
- Standard and fair grading system worked out.

4. Language

- Correct in grammar and spelling.
- Reasonably colloquial and friendly.
- Good style; clear (especially in second language).
- Correct difficulty level for students.
- Readability tested with a formula or with comprehension tests.
- Human interest sustained.
- Inclusive, non-discriminatory language.

5. Adjunct Materials (textbooks, cassettes, etc.)

- Must be well integrated and not confusing to students.
- Textbooks must be subjected to the same readability tests as course materials, and should be demonstrated to be understandable to the particular student group.
- Cassettes should generally not be long lectures, but built around interviews, drama, discussions, etc.

6. Layout and Appearance

- Specific standards may be set concerning number and length of lessons, amount of reading and assignments to be set with each lesson, etc.
- Specific standards needed as to size and shape of books, types of cover, paper used, etc.
- Covers strong enough to withstand normal use among student group.
- Reasonably attractive, but not overly-costly books.
- Books must open flat for writing in.
- Specifications needed re type size and style—larger type for less educated people or for older folk likely to have eyesight problems.
- Ample white space; avoid crammed print.
- Break up print with pictures, "boxes," diagrams, maps, etc.
- Pictures or drawings must be contextualized and meaningful to the student group.

7. Tutors' Guide

- Provide a general tutors' handbook for the entire program, with grading guide, information on curriculum, materials, seminar leading, etc.
- Provide also a tutor's guide specific to each subject, giving fairly detailed guidelines on the conduct of each seminar session, with ideas for discussion, reinforcement, and enrichment of learning through interesting learning methods. Answers to quizzes, exams, and other exercises should be given, with grading guidelines for each. Notes of areas likely to prove difficult for students. Suggestions for local application of material learned.

- Guides should include materials needed for teaching, e.g. sufficient copies of script for a short skit or drama, large pictures to be used in teaching, cassette to be played in class.

8. Testing Materials

- Ideally, the materials should be tested in a first draft form with a number of TEE students before being accepted by the TEE program as a whole and before being published in more permanent form. Results of testing—student grades and reactions—should be reported. Needed adjustments should be made.
- Early editions in less expensive format and materials.

Experiential Learning

Most of what anyone knows or is able to do has been learned from experience. It is only necessary to reflect on how we learned to speak or understand language or to behave appropriately with others to realize this. However, it appears that as people grow older, they frequently become less sensitive to that which is new or different. Our learning ability is turned off. Later schooling takes over. At least we come to identify learning with what we do in and for school. Yet we still do learn many things through experience, though often we don't notice we have learned. For instance, if a person takes a new job, there are all sorts of unwritten rules about how to behave in that particular organization, how they do things, how people relate to one another, etc., and we don't feel comfortable until we have learned these rules.

When we are presented with a new situation, we size it up and respond according to the ways we have learned previously. This response may be inappropriate. For instance, in ministry there may be activities that are necessary that have not been cultivated before. A good example is listening. What do we "hear" when someone is talking? Do we listen in order to formulate a response, a defense if we are being challenged, or an excuse? Or possibly we listen to respond with a similar story or episode in our lives or the life of a friend. Do we listen to understand how the other person feels, whether there is anger, bitterness, frustration, loneliness or pleading? To minister well to others, that is, to serve, it may be necessary to learn ways of listening that are new to us. We need to sharpen our ability to learn.

Not only do we need to become more aware of our need to learn, and how we can use experience to learn, we need systematically and intentionally to broaden our experience. A Christian who is committed to serve others may encounter new and unusual circumstances, and new issues will come into focus. One may be asked to speak or pray in public. It may be necessary to teach classes, to visit people who are sick or dying. These and many other situations a Christian faces may be threatening because we do not know how to respond appropriately. In TEE people need to learn how to minister effectively. How can they best gain experience and learn from it?

TEE offers the possibility of extensive and valuable learning. The participants are active, committed Christians, and they have plenty of experiences from which to learn. Also they study courses that provide valuable information. Unless the material in the courses connects with the day to day experience of the students' life and ministry, the most valuable learning does not take place. How then can they learn from experience and connect it with their theological study materials?

The purpose of the TEE seminar is to provide the connection between the material in books, lectures, tapes, etc. and experience in life and ministry. For this reason, facilitators of TEE centers should be people with as wide experience as possible, along with the cognitive information of courses, to help participants see and make the connections.

Step One

Faculty and students should review each course of study in light of the following questions.

1. List the ways each course utilizes experiences that are appropriate for ministry, e.g. pastoral visits, evangelistic contacts, visiting or living with people who have particular needs, in order to understand their perspective.

2. What means do participants use to observe and record their experiences, e.g log or journal, special pages for reports, check lists, etc.?

3. At what points in the schedule of the seminars are pertinent experiences brought into focus and discussed with respect to the text and workbook materials?

4. What exercises are used to sharpen peoples' sensitivities to others in observing, listening, inquiring appropriately, to gain understanding?

5. Do the facilitators systematically draw out students' experiences and help the students make the connections between the biblical-theological material studied and their experience?

6. Are the aspects of life frequently overlooked brought into focus and the biblical-theological implications discussed, e.g. social and financial problems and issues, wealth, health, environment, political issues?

Step Two

Plan ways in each course of study to include the appropriate aspects of the above questions. While not all modes or types of experience are germane to every course, try to distribute the activities so that over the whole course of study a great variety are included. Focus especially on the kinds of experiences that are important in ministry.

Step Three

Gather faculty and students at the end of each course of study to review the questions, consider how well experience was integrated in the academic work, and determine what was learned. Take into account any new suggestions; ask how they might fit in the course; indicate in what seminar they might best be introduced.

TEE Seminars

Ideally, TEE seminars (also known as tutorials) are held weekly or as often as possible. Where necessary the "external studies" model of one or more "residential schools" of a weekend to a month in duration may be substituted for the more desirable regular class meetings. Experience suggests that more students drop out and group cohesion is lost when seminars are held less frequently than once a month.

These seminars are NOT lectures. They are times for interaction and for learning experiences not possible in the individual study mode. TEE utilizes self-study materials rather than lectures for most of the cognitive input. Many TEE programs have found their seminars were greatly enhanced by providing carefully designed tutor guides for each course.

Questions for Evaluation of TEE Seminars

1. How frequently are seminars held in the various TEE centers? How long do they last? A minimum of one hour per subject per week or its equivalent at less frequent intervals is usually suggested. Is this sufficient to build group cohesion and to achieve the interactive objectives of the course?

2. Do visiting tutors take time to build relationships in local centers, e.g. by staying on for coffee or a meal, visiting, or perhaps over-nighting in students' homes?

3. Are seminars real times of interaction, not lectures?

4. Are tutors (also called "facilitators"), center leaders, etc. trained in facilitative skills and group dynamics? Are training programs repeated periodically for new tutors?

5. Is there always adequate discussion and critical reflection?

6. Do seminars consisted of little else but discussion or utilize a range of teaching-learning methods?

7. Does the program provide:

   • a general tutor's handbook for the whole program?

   • a tutor's subject guide for each individual course with practical suggestions for each seminar?

8. How well do you feel the seminars integrate the material studied at home and the actual lives and ministries of the students? How would you determine if such integration has occurred?

A Checklist of Ideas for Teaching and Learning

Some learning methods can be used in the study materials and also in the seminars. Others are only suited to the seminar situation. Further, some methods are well suited with adaptation to any academic level, whereas others are best used at either a higher or a lower level.

Each TEE program may like to build its own checklist of suitable methods, using the following as a starting point and adding other methods as appropriate. Participants could then check off those you are already using or those they would like to try. The checklist is useful in designing tutor's subject guides with specific suggestions and materials for use in TEE seminars.

• Group discussion (plenary and "buzz" sessions should be part of all TEE seminars but not the only component)

• Small group research projects, with materials provided.

• Lecturettes or seminar papers presented by students for group discussion.

• Group projects and presentations.

• Demonstration lessons (show students how to do something, then let them try).

• Group excursions.

• Action-Reflection projects.

- Group Bible studies (use a variety of methods).
- Films and videos (documentaries and movies) followed by discussion (with prepared discussion guides).
- Cassette presentations.
- Visiting speakers (talk or interview with question time) (use sparingly since lectures are not normally a part of the seminar).
- Filmstrips and slide sets, with or without cassette scripts.
- Panel discussions.
- Debates.
- Discussions built around a quotation put on the board.
- Case studies.
- Simulation games, role plays, and board games.
- Various forms of drama—formal, semi-formal, spontaneous, mime.
- Scripted and partly-scripted skits.
- "Radio plays" (voices only).
- Puppet dramas.
- Group expression by making posters, charts, collages, videos, slide-tape presentations, etc.
- Group work on coordinated murals, time-lines, etc.
- Spontaneous artwork, writing of poems and stories, composition of music, modelling, etc. in response to certain themes or concerns (group or individual) (good for reaching affective objectives).
- Creative dance.
- Multi-media presentations by students.
- Use of traditional art-forms and media in local culture.
- Community development or social action task forces.
- Brainstorming as a form of problem-solving.
- Community research in some problem area.

Questions to Ask about Teaching and Learning Methods

1. Which of the above methods can be used in TEE programs among marginal literates, or by TEE students undertaking projects alongside the poor?

2. How can you determine which learning methods are appropriate to different subjects in your curriculum?

3. What traditional methods of learning (formal and non-formal) are found in your culture? Which of these might be used or adapted for TEE?

4. What methods would be best in your area for teaching:
   - Cognitive Objectives.
   - Affective Objectives (attitudes, values, spiritual formation).
   - Skill objectives.

Developing Reflective Thinking and Problem-Solving Skills

Since this is a crucial area in Christian formation, participants may like to try listing practical ways of cultivating these skills in various courses. Following is a list developed by other theological teachers; it overlaps with our Teaching and Learning Methods Checklist above.

- Discussion
- Debates
- Panels
- Case studies
- Simulations
- Puzzles
- Brainstorming
- "Socratic" teaching
- Essay writing

- Group problem-solving exercises
- Student presentations
- Action-reflection projects
- Values clarification exercises
- "What would happen . . . ?" hypotheticals
- Translation and paraphrasing tasks
- Inductive Bible studies
- Exercises in ordering sequences, matching, categorizing, assessing evidence, etc.

Sample Student Evaluation Sheet for TEE Seminars

The following questionnaire is adapted from a Latin American evaluation sheet given to students to obtain their feedback on TEE seminars.

1. How did you find the fellowship among all the students in your TEE group?

    Excellent   Very Good   Good   Fair   Poor

2. Did you feel the seminars motivated the group to Christian service?

    Yes   Somewhat   No   Not sure

3. Did you personally feel motivated and inspired by the group sessions?

    Yes   Somewhat   No

4. Were the tutor and the group able to provide answers to students' questions and help with the resolution of problems?

    Yes   Somewhat   No   Not sure

5. How would you describe the discussion times you had in group sessions?

    Excellent   Very Good   Good   Fair   Poor

6. How do you feel the lessons and assignments were applied to the ministry and life of the students?

    Very well   Well   Fairly well   A little   Not at all

7. What learning methods (in addition to discussion) were used in your group?

8. In what ways could the seminars have been improved?

9. What did you like best about the seminars?

10. Any other comments?

Accessibility of TEE Programs

Many TEE programs have made theological education far more accessible to all sectors of the church than ever before. Some have intentionally focused on specific academic levels and constituencies. All may want to review their goals, theological foundations, and educational approaches in relation to this question of accessibility, which may in fact be the most important question we have to deal with.

In recent discussion about ministry—as in discussion about health care, development, and other fields— there has been a major shift toward local leaders as the primary agents of service and change. We have rediscovered in the Bible God's compassion for the poor and oppressed; Jesus sought out and was received by sinners, women, children, the poor, and even foreigners; for all his genius Paul recognized that God chooses not the powerful, noble, and wise but rather the weak, foolish, and despised. So we must ask ourselves whether our TEE programs are really accessible to marginalized people in our own contexts.

The following exercise may be used by theological educators, students, and church people to focus on the critical issue of accessibility. Participants may all work together or divide into groups and later share their findings in plenary. Background information about the TEE program, the church(es) served, the general population, and geography may be distributed prior to the session or at the outset. Discussion of findings should lead to recommendations, further reflection, and later evaluations.

Step One

Consider first these factors: geography, academic level, and economics.

- Where are the present extension centers located and where are additional centers needed to provide reasonable access to all regions of the church?
- What academic levels are now offered and what levels should be offered to enable all socioeconomic sectors of the church to participate?
- How reasonable are the costs of the program and how could persons of limited resources be helped?

Step Two

Now consider these more subtle factors of accessibility: motivation, language and culture, study methods, seminar style, scheduling of assignments and meetings, etc. In some cultural contexts women still feel uncomfortable in meetings for discussion with men, as do indigenous people with persons of the dominant culture, or even in some cases younger people with older persons.

- Can these differences and disadvantages be overcome by using different role models, methods, and styles of meeting?
- Have representatives of marginalized groups participated in the design and preparation of the study materials?
- Can our differences become an important, intentional dimension of the learning experience, in which the strengths as well as the weaknesses of each group become the concern of all?

Step Three

The dichotomy between ordained and unordained leaders may seem insuperable, but there are strong biblical-theological and sociological-ideological reasons to continue the struggle to recover and implement the Reformation vision of a common, universal priesthood of all believers.

- Does the extension program focus on ministry in the world as the primary mission of the church, in which the laity are the primary agents?
- Do the extension program participants realize that they are called to incarnate the Gospel, create contextual theology, and recreate the church in their own contexts—not simply to repeat watered down versions of imported, high level theologies and serve as assistants to the pastor?

Assignments and Assessment

We are using the term assessment here to refer specifically to the assessment of students' work. Evaluation is a much broader term and refers to the overall program and its various components. Evaluation also involves a judgment with respect to the value of the program in terms of its relation to ministry, church, and life. Our focus here is on assessment of students.

What Are the Functions of Assessment of Students' Work?

1. Teaching: Formative assessment (undertaken during a course) enables the student to learn from assignments and to diagnose weaknesses and misunderstandings. It also helps the teacher in these same ways, so s/he can in turn assist the students more.

2. Grading: Assessment determines whether or not a student has reached a satisfactory standard in terms of an award, entry to another study program, employment, etc.

3. Understanding of the course: Assessment helps the student understand the aims of the course and the standards expected.

4. Course design: Assessment of student learning should reveal whether the study materials and seminars are achieving their objectives and provide clear indications where changes should be made.

How Often Should Assessment Take Place?

Summative assessment means that one final exam or major assignment is all that is required for the course. The problem with this older form of assessment is that by the time the student receives the results, it is too late to learn much from the feedback—the course is already over. Also, it is common for the students to receive very little helpful feedback in this kind of assessment, particularly when it takes the form of an external examination which is not returned to the student.

Progressive or continual assessment, sometimes called "formative evaluation," is widely thought to be preferable today, since students are able to note their progress, learn from the feedback, and work at a steady pace throughout the term. With summative assessment there is a temptation to leave much of the study till the last moment. A final exam may be taken on a day when a student is feeling ill or nervous, and so may not adequately reflect real knowledge and ability.

Teachers and students may consider the following ways to time assessment and discuss which would be best for their needs. They may want to list the advantages and disadvantages of each alternative.

- only at the conclusion of the course
- on completion of each major unit of work
- at important points in the syllabus
- once each term or semester
- at random
- at every TEE class
- at regular intervals (weekly, monthly, bi-monthly)

Who Should Assess?

Participants may consider each of the following, note which of these are now doing assessments, and ask which additional ones they would like to try.

- the tutor
- an outside examining body
- a church ordination committee
- a committee of parishioners (e.g. with field education assignments in the church)
- a prospective employer (or an existing employer)

- a teaching team
- the designer of the TEE course materials
- groups of peers
- the whole class (e.g. when a student preaches in a homiletics class)
- the student (self-evaluation)

What Sources of Information Can Be Used?

Participants may consider each of the following sources or methods, note which of these are not being used, discuss their advantages and disadvantages, and ask which additional ones they would like to introduce.

- tests and exams (designed by course writer, tutor, church body, employer, or outside examiner)
- various other types of assignments (designed by any of the above)
- standardized tests
- self-reports
- reports by advisors and employers
- reports by peers
- assessment sheets used by whole class
- practical work (observed by tutor)
- questionnaires, rating scales
- practical work recorded on cassette or video
- summary portfolio of past achievements
- comparison with group "norms" or averages (norm-referenced assessment)
- comparison with set performance criteria and standards (criterion-referenced assessment)

Various tests and assignments may be graded as norm-referenced or as criterion-referenced tests. One form of criterion-referenced assessment is "mastery learning" where high standards of achievement can be set and good teaching and learning methods designed to ensure that most students will in fact reach these standards. This approach is good with practical subjects where the minimum standard is a high one. (Compare a clear example such as learning to fly a plane. Is it good enough if students learn 50% of the skills and knowledge needed to do this?)

Assessment needs to be made as non-threatening as possible for people of little formal education who may find tests and exams very daunting and essays nearly impossible to write. In some TEE programs for lay leaders there may be no need for formal assessment at all. In other cases it may be entirely criterion-referenced in terms of practical skills learned. The student either learns to do something or not—without need for grades.

Questions for Discussion on Student Assessment in TEE

1. Are all major course objectives clearly stated and then assessed in some way?

2. Are cognitive, affective, and skill objectives included in good balance?

3. Do all assignments, tests, etc. relate in some definite way to the objectives of the course?

4. Are course priorities reflected in the weighting of marks assigned to various assignments?

5. If much reading is required, how does assessment ensure that this has been done? Many students do not read required books except insofar as they must do so to write assignments or take exams. To ensure necessary reading is completed, it often helps to give some assignments on that reading, to build discussion times around reading done before class, or to have students sign on an honor system that they have conscientiously completed the reading.

6. Have opportunities been provided for self-evaluation by the student, at least in some courses?

7. Do assessment procedures encourage reflection and a variety of mental and, where appropriate, physical processes? Do they minimize requirements of rote learning, copying (with slight changes) from textbooks, and other non-educative processes?

8. Do the courses encourage group as well as individual assignments, especially in group oriented cultures?

9. If society encourages cooperation and discourages competition, or if this is considered to be a more Christian approach anyway, do the assignments take this into account?

10. Are the amount and level of assessment well suited to the students' educational levels and to the time available?

11. Can students see the purpose and value of each assignment?

12. Are the assessment procedures valid, i.e. do they measure what they are supposed to measure? Are they reliable, i.e. do they measure this consistently?

13. If the students are marginal literates, are most of their assignments practical, not burdening them with lots of time-consuming written work and with reading they find difficult to handle?

14. Are the assessment procedures as relaxed and non-threatening as possible?

15. Is assessment well-timed and coordinated with assessment in any other TEE subjects students may be doing, so all their work does not pile up at one time?

16. Is assessment always fair? If certain parts of the course are used for testing, are they important areas? Are "trick" questions based on obscure details avoided?

17. Are all aspects of assessment made clear to students from the outset?

18. Are assignments varied? Do they allow for choice? For different ways of being assessed? (Some write well, others do better on oral tests.)

Obstacles, Delays, and Dropouts

Theological education by extension offers a wide front door that provides access for many more people than could in the past enter theological studies. It also offers a wide back door so that many can drop out or discontinue their studies for any reasons. Both the wide front door and the wide back door are important, for they increase significantly the probability that those who continue, graduate, and are ordained or otherwise identified for specific ministries are really called, equipped, and qualified for those ministries. Extension studies require extraordinary discipline and dedication, for in most cases these students continue to carry a full load of responsibilities in their homes, employment, churches, and communities. There are many obstacles that can delay and prolong the process; many good candidates may be forced to drop out temporarily or permanently due to illness, job transfer, and other vicissitudes of life.

TEE organizers, teachers, students, and church leaders need to make every effort to facilitate the learning process for such people through appropriate resources and accompaniment and to avoid unnecessary additional obstacles and delays through faulty materials, seminars, administration, and other services. One way to do so is to gather feedback from students who have dropped out of the program, postponed further study, or slowed their progress. This may be difficult to achieve, but it should be an important way to evaluate the program.

What follows is a questionnaire on deterrents to TEE study. Persons interested in using this questionnaire as a tool for evaluation of their programs will want to examine carefully all the questions, make changes that suit their own situation, and consider how best to implement the survey. They may want to add a section to gather information about the respondents (e.g. age, sex, marital status, previous schooling, occupation, employment, denomination, church responsibilities) and about their participation in the program (e.g. motivation, year enrolled, courses completed). These data may later be tabulated and correlated with the dropout factors listed below. It may be useful to use the same questionnaire with a number of successful students and/or graduates in order to compare their responses with the others. The questionnaire may be distributed with a letter expressing concern for the students' ongoing life and ministry, avoiding any criticism of those who have dropped out or behind, and requesting their help in improving the program. The survey may bring both just and unjust criticism of the program, and it may encourage some to renew their studies.

DETERRENTS to T.E.E. STUDIES

Please circle only one indication for each of the following statements. Circle **SA** if you **strongly agree** that this factor has influenced your decision to drop out of the course or program, to become inactive, or to delay and make difficult its completion. Circle **SD** if you **strongly disagree** that this factor has influenced your decision. Circle **U** if you are **uncertain**. Circle **A** or **D** to indicate mild **agreement** or **disagreement**.

	Agree				Disagree
1. The courses and program did not meet my needs.	SA	A	U	D	SD
2. The courses were not useful or practical.	SA	A	U	D	SD
3. I wanted something more specific; these courses were too general.	SA	A	U	D	SD
4. The courses were not interesting.	SA	A	U	D	SD
5. The quality of the courses was poor.	SA	A	U	D	SD
6. The level of the course requirements was too high for me.	SA	A	U	D	SD
7. My skills and habits of study were not good.	SA	A	U	D	SD
8. I did not have a good background in the subject matter of the courses.	SA	A	U	D	SD

	Agree			Disagree	
9. I did not get much encouragement from family and friends.	SA	A	U	D	SD
10. I felt I was too old to take the course.	SA	A	U	D	SD
11. I did not like to study.	SA	A	U	D	SD
12. I was afraid of not being able to fulfill the course requirements.	SA	A	U	D	SD
13. I could not afford the cost of tuition and books.	SA	A	U	D	SD
14. My church could not provide enough financial assistance.	SA	A	U	D	SD
15. I did not have time to study.	SA	A	U	D	SD
16. The time required to complete the courses was too long.	SA	A	U	D	SD
17. I did not receive enough orientation about how to study.	SA	A	U	D	SD
18. Difficulty in writing assignments.	SA	A	U	D	SD
19. Difficulty in finding the books, course materials, and other resources.	SA	A	U	D	SD
20. It took too long to receive feedback from tutors or professors.	SA	A	U	D	SD
21. I did not receive answers to my papers or letters.	SA	A	U	D	SD
22. The feedback I got was too critical and negative.	SA	A	U	D	SD
23. Little support and guidance to improve my work.	SA	A	U	D	SD
24. Lack of clarity on what I was expected to do.	SA	A	U	D	SD
25. Little availability or lack or communication with tutors.	SA	A	U	D	SD
26. The course activities and program were too rigid with little room for personal interests and needs.	SA	A	U	D	SD
27. I did not agree with the content and theology of the courses.	SA	A	U	D	SD
28. I did not agree with the theology of the institution running the program.	SA	A	U	D	SD
29. I had difficulty doing assignments that involved practical work in the church.	SA	A	U	D	SD
30. I did not like the assignments that involved practical work in the community.	SA	A	U	D	SD
31. Personal problems (physical, vocational, emotional, spiritual).	SA	A	U	D	SD
32. Family problems (e.g. not enough time to spend with the family).	SA	A	U	D	SD
33. My church or pastor did not like the theological orientation of the program.	SA	A	U	D	SD
34. Problems with or in the church.	SA	A	U	D	SD

Please add comments about any aspect of your experience as a TEE student that was not included in this questionnaire or that you want to explain more fully.

Graduates: Source of Evaluation

The best source of evaluation of a program of theological education could be the graduates. They have been intimately connected with the program; they have received its benefits. They have continued in ministry and are in contact with the grass roots situation. They may be aware of their strengths and weaknesses, and they could provide information about how to best make up for any lack they experienced. Particularly, if they have been active in the various forms of ministry, they can provide a perspective that others cannot. Therefore, it is worth looking to the graduates for help in critically analyzing and reformulating the program.

There are a number of ways in which this might be done.

- **Questionnaires**. These can be distributed through the mail or at gatherings of the graduates for some special event, etc. One problem with the mailed questionnaire is that the response rate is generally poor and may only get responses from those who are antagonistic.

- **Interviews**. Interviews can often be the best form for obtaining detailed information, for not only can a standard set of questions be asked, but certain ones can be followed up with general discussion to receive more detailed information on critical issues. The major obstacle is the amount of time and cost it takes if a good overall picture is to be obtained.

- **Conference**. A convention or conference might be held, inviting the graduates to come for the purpose of discussing and evaluating the plan and program. It can be held as a separate event or planned to coincide with another when all will be present. Again the problem might be cost, as well as the difficulty in allowing all participants to express themselves, not permitting the meeting to be dominated by a few.

In all these forms, the continual problem is to learn what in the theological program was relevant, useful, and helpful and what was not. There will of course be quite different perceptions of what is important, and these must be heard, though not all will be useful. For instance, many will bring up issues that were not adequately handled. The question may be, Should they have been treated at this point in the student's life. Theological preparation cannot be exhaustive in the sense of providing all the resources that the students will need throughout their life and ministry. The preparation should be focused on providing tools, background skills, and information so that they can continue to study, reflect, and refine and develop skills during their whole career. Thus there might emerge from the evaluation a list of themes to treat that is much too large and detailed to be covered in the curriculum.

Another consideration to take into account is that those who studied many years earlier may have forgotten what the program was like, and the program may have changed in the interim so that many of their observations may already be obsolete. This will be especially true for those who did all their studies before beginning ministry. They may not have had enough experience to allow them to relate significant parts of the program to their life. Therefore, as students might have focused on issues that were not really relevant for active ministry, and they may not have paid attention to those that were. This could lead to a very distorted memory of the program.

Education also serves to provide background information that is never used directly. As one professor put it, "education is what is left when you have forgotten all you learned." That is to say, in order to continue, participants need certain information; later, they study and build upon this, expand it, but never specifically return to use the details earlier learned. There are many fields of learning in which participants will later use only a fraction of the total area of study. This is because the initial program of study in any field must be wide and general; this provides the basis on which people can branch into many specific activities. One may end up as a counsellor, another as a preacher, another works in administration, another in teaching, another in evangelism, etc. There will clearly be many things in common, and the basis for their work may be similar, but they each must learn more as they concentrate. The theological program cannot provide all they will ever need. This fact needs to be considered by those critiquing the program.

The graduates may also have gone through major ideological shifts, a conversion, a series of experiences that have left them frustrated, or they might have reacted against the earlier stance. All these could affect their point of view, their critique of the program. These shifts occur not only to individuals, but also to institutions, so that the disjuncture between the institution and the graduate may be due to changes in the institution. Then the question is, Is the present evaluation appropriate? Has new information been revealed that might be important, or is it irrelevant? This judgment can only be rendered after hearing and reflecting on the comments of the graduate. Of course, diverse opinions may exist within the controlling body even after the evaluation, so that further reflection would be required to come to a consensus.

Following are some questions that might be considered by the graduates.

What information did you study in your courses that was never used in your ministry? Why was it not used?

What materials do you now consider significant? Why?

In what ways have you made use of the following studies?

- **Exegesis.** Have you made continual use, some, not at all?

- **Inductive Studies of the Bible,** of other books?

- Has the method of learning in TEE influenced your methods of teaching/learning?

- **Church History/Theology.** Has it been a source of illustrations? For understanding theology in context? For teaching classes in the church? Other uses?

- **Homiletics/Preaching.** Have you used what you studied, or returned to it for help? What parts have been helpful? What parts have not been useful?

- **Pastoral Work.** Have the courses been applicable? What parts were most valuable, what least?

- Did you learn how to learn? Have you continued some form of disciplined study?

- What other aspects of your studies have you made use of, and which have you not found useful?

Faculty Selection and Development

The term faculty usually means "teaching staff" and, in the specific case of TEE, it includes both course designers and tutors. Here it refers not only to personnel exclusively dedicated to teaching activities. In the case of many Two-Thirds World countries ("Where the harvest is plentiful but the laborers are few"), professors and tutors do administrative work, and administrative workers take teaching functions. In conclusion, all those who have an explicit function in the program, whether fully or partially, whether as tutors in a center or as professors and course designers, whether with theologically specialized training or with more general or limited academic formation, may be included.

FACULTY SELECTION

Exercise 1

Mark those criteria which your program usually takes into account in the selection of faculty. You may then reflect on why the criteria not marked are not usually considered and why the marked criteria are the ones generally used.

__ academic degrees

__ academic publications

__ experience in adult education

__ denominational background

__ present church involvement

__ social class background

__ sex

__ teaching experience

__ pastoral experience

__ experience in TEE

__ theological background

__ economic demands

__ ethnic origin

__ nationality

__ availability to travel to centers

__ experience and willingness to work at grass roots levels

__ willingness to accept the goals, methods, and theological assumptions of the program

__ other (specify):

Exercise 2

Mark the procedures generally used in processing applications for faculty positions. Discuss why those procedures are generally used, rather than those that were not marked.

__ candidate interviews with the selection committee

__ candidate interviews with the faculty

__ candidate interviews with the students

__ lecture presentation by the candidate

__ teaching session by the candidate

__ writing a unit or section for curriculum materials

__ written statement of faith

__ other (specify):

Questions for further reflection:

1. Who selects new faculty members?

2. Who decides who makes the selection?

3. Who decides how the selection should be made?

4. Does the selection process require open consultation with others involved in the program who are not members of the selection committee? If so, who decides who will be consulted? What form does the consultation take?

FACULTY DEVELOPMENT

TEE programs may want to reflect on the continuing development of their faculty members. The areas of development should be in the same areas in which the TEE program aims to develop its students. There should be some congruence between student and faculty development.

If the main purpose of a TEE program is to offer a high level academic program, then what matters most will be the academic development of its faculty. Considerations about faculty involvement in church work or about their personal devotional practices may be seen as an intrusion into their private lives. If the main purpose of the TEE program is to train pastors and leaders for their practical-ministerial vocations in their churches, then faculty involvement in some kind of church work may be not only desired but also required. Still other TEE programs may be concentrated in the development of the spiritual-devotional life of their students. In this case more attention will be given to the spiritual-devotional qualities of faculty members. Most TEE programs will claim a combination of these three areas, namely, academic, ministerial, and spiritual development.

By reflecting on the following questions, a balance can be sought and action can be taken to strengthen the weaker areas of faculty development. These questions have been elaborated with reference to TEE programs which are related to or have emanated from theological colleges and seminaries; church-based programs may not find every question applicable. In any case, it is up to users of this tool to select those questions most relevant to their own needs and purpose, and to add others as they wish.

Area I: Academic Development

1. What are the minimum academic requirements that the TEE program demands of course designers and of its tutors in regional centers?

2. What are the minimum and maximum teaching loads that the TEE program allows its faculty to carry?

3. Does the TEE program see as necessary a continuing up-dating of its faculty? If not, Why not?

4. Check the following list and mark the opportunities your program provides for the development either of course designers or tutors or both.

   a. Our TEE program gives its faculty sabbatical periods for writing a book, for taking relevant courses at the graduate level, etc.

   b. It allows faculty salaried time for development in their own or other academic fields.

   c. It requires of its faculty:
   ___research work
   ___attendance at professional conferences
   ___writing of books
   ___writing of articles
   ___trying out different teaching topics
   ___trying out different teaching methods
   ___other (specify) _____

   d. It promotes team-teaching of courses and/or co-writing of curricular materials for TEE.

e. It supports and sponsors further formation of faculty by:
   ___channeling scholarship funds for faculty members
   ___offering workshops for tutors and course writers
   ___holding periodic colloquia on relevant books, events, etc.
   ___encouraging faculty to take courses in other areas
   ___promoting participation in seminars, consultations, etc.
   ___subscribing to relevant journals

f. It requires regular book reviews in which faculty share recent reading.

g. It organizes faculty exchange programs with other theological institutions.

Now answer the following questions:
   · Have the opportunities your program has provided been satisfactory? Why? Why not?
   · Do you think it will be possible to implement some of the activities you did not mark?
      · If so, What are some of the changes or decisions that should be made?
      · If not, Why not?

5. What kinds of criteria does the TEE program use to "categorize" its faculty? On what bases are seniority and salary scales determined? How does this ranking of staff affect intra-faculty and faculty-student relations?

Area II: Ministerial Development

1. How do the program organizers understand the work of their tutors and course designers? Is it understood as a ministry strictly located within the framework of the program or as a ministry that can be extended and transferred to other contexts, e.g. churches, institutions, and/or communities?

2. Are faculty members encouraged to accept calls from churches and other organizations to lecture, lead workshops, or participate in different events? Does the program promote and sponsor this kind of faculty experience?

3. Does the program encourage or require faculty involvement in a church? If so, How is that experience integrated into the program? If not, Why not?

4. Is the faculty open to students' problems other than academic? Does the program promote genuine relationships between faculty and students and among the faculty members themselves? How do students and teachers address each other?

5. Does the program support or promote faculty participation in social organizations (e.g. human rights committees, cooperatives, unions, etc.) at local, regional, and national levels? If so, how does that experience inform and affect the program? If not, why not?

Area III: Spiritual Development

1. How is "spirituality" defined and understood within the program? Is it solely a matter of morality, private devotions, church activity, and personal conduct? Does it extend to interpersonal relationships in the light of Christ's example? Does it cover Christian commitment to and involvement in peace, justice, and environmental movements in the larger society?

2. Does the TEE program promote a fellowship of love, worship, and prayer among faculty members and students? In what specific ways is fellowship promoted?

3. Are there programmed activities throughout the year in which faculty members have responsibilities as worship leaders, preachers, communion officers, etc.?

4. How are the conflicts among faculty members dealt with? How much do personal interests intervene in the decisions the faculty make about different aspects of the program?

5. What kinds of relationships exist between faculty and students? Do they create gaps between those who know and those who do not know? Do they allow students to express themselves in a free and creative way? Do they see the teaching-learning process as a two-way process?

Facilitator Roles and Student Roles

An essential component of the TEE model is the regular seminar meeting, which is designed to clarify and deepen cognitive learning and integrate it with the on-going experiential learning through group discussion and other forms of interaction. Thus it is very important to clarify and strengthen the roles of facilitators and students at these seminar meetings. Many people have traditionally thought of these roles as one continuum, with the teacher at one end and the students at the other. According to this understanding, when the teacher takes an active role, the students must follow passively, and vice versa.

TEACHER———————————— STUDENT

A more dynamic understanding is expressed through the following diagram, in which the roles are separate but interrelated.

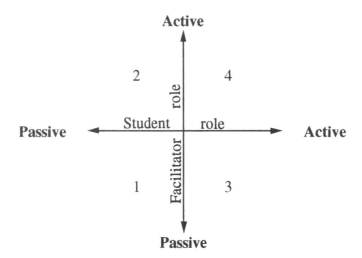

In some TEE programs both students and facilitators are relatively passive, simply following a routine established by set materials, set exercises, set evaluations, etc., as in quadrant 1 of the diagram. In other programs the teacher may be creative and the students passive, as in quadrant 2. Or the students may be very active and the facilitator passive, as in quadrant 3. The ideal is to develop a dynamic process in which facilitator and students both engage actively in the design, leadership, and entire process of the seminar meetings, which will assure a high level of motivation, maximize learning, and equip all the participants for future leadership in ministry, as in quadrant 4.

Step One

Participants (in groups and/or plenary) may reflect on their experiences in their current TEE program and in other contexts in order to evaluate the level of dynamic participation and effective learning. They may wish to make a list of the factors that have contributed to this process: basing discussion on material studied previously, relating study with the practice of ministry, openness to questions and answers by all participants, encouraging expression and debate of differences, acceptance of negative feelings, variety of activities, mutual pastoral care, etc. This list could be shaped into a check-list for periodic evaluation by local TEE groups to encourage them to take responsibility for improvement.

Step Two

Participants may wish to work out detailed lists of the functions of the seminar meeting, the role of the facilitator, and the role of the students. In some contexts it may be difficult to move from a traditional authoritarian pattern (the teacher knows the right questions and the right answers) toward an increasingly communitarian pattern (facilitator and students together identify critical questions and work out significant answers). In other situations it may soon become evident that all are facilitators and learners.

Step Three

Participants may wish to explore additional, special activities that might deepen their relationships, take their learnings into the churches, provide opportunities for recreation and retreat, etc.

Student Evaluation of Courses and Facilitators

In the past theological educators have generally considered evaluation to be a process by which they judged how well students learned what they were taught. Examination and grading at the end of each course were thus a kind of trial, and it could be very traumatic for students. More recently we have begun to see that the lack of learning may be primarily the fault of the teacher and the study materials. So it is important to develop instruments to evaluate the courses and the facilitators, and the students can play a critical role in this regard. In any case, whether teachers are evaluating students or vice versa, our primary concern is to improve the learning process.

Following is a sample form for students to fill out at the end of a course. This particular form was prepared by students and teachers of a seminary which has both residential and extension programs, so some points may not be relevant for TEE. Students should fill out such forms anonymously and turn them in directly to the administration, which should tabulate the results and review them with the professor and/or course designer.

FORM FOR STUDENT EVALUATION OF COURSE AND PROFESSORS

Students should read through the entire questionnaire, omit any points that are not applicable for the specific course being evaluated, consider carefully the sense of the other points, indicate the degree of achievement for each, and add additional observations at the end of each section. Rate each item on the scale by checking the appropriate space. The values are: Deficient, Passing, Good, Very good and Excellent.

	Def.	Pass	Good	V.good	Excel
THE COURSE _____					
Objectives					
1. Objectives are adequate for the level of the course.	—	—	—	—	—
2. They are expressed clearly and concisely.	—	—	—	—	—
3. They were discussed at the beginning of the course.	—	—	—	—	—
4. To what degree were they achieved?	—	—	—	—	—
Planning					
1. At the beginning of the course the syllabus was discussed.	—	—	—	—	—
2. The amount of work required was appropriate for the theme and level of the course.	—	—	—	—	—
3. Time was adequately distributed to cover the topics and activities.	—	—	—	—	—
Contents and Methodology					
1. The course contents are appropriate for the objectives.	—	—	—	—	—
2. The contents are appropriate for the pastoral needs of the region/nation.	—	—	—	—	—
3. The assignments were pertinent for the course content and objectives.	—	—	—	—	—
4. The tests/exams were coherent with the contents and objectives.	—	—	—	—	—
5. The teaching/learning methods were coherent with the contents and objectives.	—	—	—	—	—
6. The class dynamics were varied.	—	—	—	—	—

	Def.	Pass	Good	V.good	Excel

7. If a blackboard was used, it helped understanding of the topic. — — — — —

8. The professor's commentaries on students reports contributed to learning. — — — — —

9. The course stimulated creative and critical thinking. — — — — —

10. The bibliography aided comprehension of the subject. — — — — —

11. The required bibliographic was obtainable. — — — — —

12. Suggestions and recommendations to improve the contents and methodology of the course:

THE FACILITATOR _____

1. Did s/he show adequate knowledge of the subject? — — — — —

2. Did s/he demonstrate interest in the course? — — — — —

3. Did s/he manage well the time in class? — — — — —

4. Was s/he punctual? — — — — —

5. Was his/her manner of speaking clear and vocabulary adequate? — — — — —

6. Did s/he review and return student assignments in good time? — — — — —

7. Did s/he prepare for class adequately? — — — — —

8. Did s/he stimulate and maintain students' interest? — — — — —

9. Did s/he manifest openness to the students and their opinions? — — — — —

10. Was s/he able to systematize his/her thoughts? — — — — —

11. Is s/he up to date on theoretical-practical progress in the field? — — — — —

12. Does s/he identify with local and regional problems/realities? — — — — —

13. Was s/he able to give pastoral guidance to the students? — — — — —

14. Was s/he able to communicate with students in and out of class? — — — — —

15. Would you enroll in another course with this professor:
with enthusiasm___, yes___, if necessary after seeking alternatives___, no___.

16. Suggestions and recommendations that you consider appropriate:

THE STUDENT

1. Indicate your level of interest in the subject, whatever the grade? — — — — —

2. Did you complete the assignments of the course? — — — — —

3. Did you participate actively in class? — — — — —

4. Did you arrive on time? — — — — —

5. What was your attendance? — — — — —

6. How much did your knowledge increase? — — — — —

7. How would you rate your own academic achievement in this course? — — — — —

8. Suggestions on any aspect of the course, the facilitator, the students, etc.

Education for Self-Development

All theological education, particularly theological education by extension, should maintain its focus on the students, who are the subject of the entire enterprise. Our concern should be directed primarily toward the quality and relevance of the students' formation for ministry, not toward the excellence of our teaching nor the prestige of our institutions.

TEE workers have long emphasized that theological institutions might in fact achieve more genuine results, in terms of formation for ministry, if they would presume to do less. They point out that the seed-bed for ministry, where leadership gifts and vocations are identified, take root, and grow, is not the seminary (which means seed-bed) but the local church. TEE seeks to strengthen, not by-pass, this dynamic process of leadership formation, to make available to local leaders the fundamental biblical and theological and pastoral tools for their self-development, and to open to them the doors of recognized ministry, lay or ordained or both. Thus TEE is an instrument for the self-development of the church.

Likewise TEE seeks to inculcate a process of self-development in each student and group of students. Professors, teachers, and/or instructors play a critical role as facilitators of their students' self-development. We sometimes refer to this process as conscientization, as students become not receptacles or deposits of knowledge imparted to them but rather conscious and increasingly capable agents of God's will for the church and the world. Self-discovery is the beginning of all true theological education, and learning to learn is its essence. Self-discovery and self-directed learning are essential to ministerial formation, which should be life-long.

Unfortunately most theological education, including TEE, has largely focused on the teacher rather than the students, the corpus of theological knowledge rather than the theological and ministerial self-formation of the church, arbitrary and abstract standards of excellence rather than the excellence of people in their witness and service. In fact the process has generally created more dependence than autonomy, dependence on professors, theologians, books, and academic and/or ecclesiastical authority. It even tends to create arrogance rather than humility with reference to the church, particularly local congregations and their members, where primary learning and ministry should take place.

TEE facilitators have a peculiar opportunity to reverse these tendencies. They will certainly want to bring to the learning process a wealth of resources from the global church and the various theological fields. But they will need to respect and nurture the autonomy of their students, to build partnerships with shared responsibility for learning, and to encourage theological-pastoral growth in the community of learners and through them among the larger communities to which they belong. This can happen if throughout the entire process the students take increasing initiative and responsibility for their own formation.

The process of developing self-guided, increasingly autonomous learners can be illustrated in various ways. Many educators use questions as a way of leading students into increasingly complex information and issues; eventually students need to learn not only how to answer such questions but also how to formulate the questions. Other educators have noted that all learning can be broken down into examples and rules or principles; students can be challenged through a progression of examples and rules to take increasing responsibility both to give examples and to define the rules or principles. Some educators make use of programmed instruction, which seeks to provide the most efficient sequences for learning; if programmed instruction is used, it should lead progressively toward independent study, which requires no further guidance. Educators often analyze their work not only in terms of learning objectives but in terms of hierarchies of learning objectives; then they build courses and curricula around logical sequences of information, concepts, and rules until they reach the level of problem-solving, at which point the students are equipped to continue on their own.

Following are three exercises which can help facilitators and students to evaluate their work in terms of learning to learn, awakening, and equipping for autonomous, life-long learning. Both facilitators and students need to ask themselves whether effective self-development is being encouraged not only throughout the theological education process but also in the congregations to which they relate.

Exercise One

Participants may discuss the above paragraphs, then consider to what degree and in what ways specific courses equip people for autonomous, ongoing learning. In preparation for this session each professor, facilitator, or course designer may be asked to prepare a description of the learning process of a specific course in these terms. As a result of this session general or specific recommendations may be drawn up.

Exercise Two

Participants may make a similar analysis of the curriculum as a whole and/or the basic academic areas. Beginning with a profile of graduates ready for ministry, they may consider to what degree and in what ways the courses and other components of the curriculum prepare people for life-long learning in ministry. This session, too, may require prior preparation and lead to recommendations that should be reviewed at a later date.

Exercise Three

Participants may examine their institution or program as a whole in terms of its relationship to local churches and their leaders and in terms of the issues raised in this material. This discussion should identify general and specific needs or problems and lead to corresponding recommendations that should be reviewed at a later date.

Appendix: Report of the San Jose Consultation

Opting for Change

Fifty theological educators from around the world gathered in San José, Costa Rica for a Consultation on Evaluation of Theological Education by Extension Programs, May 8-12, 1990. Sponsored by the Program on Theological Education of the World Council of Churches and hosted by the Latin American Biblical Seminary, this was the first time in the 28 years since the "TEE" model of theological education first appeared in Central America that representatives of the movement in Africa and Asia, Australia and the Pacific, Latin America and the Caribean, North America and Europe have had the opportunity to meet for such an evaluation. The eagerness with which the participants dealt with the challenge of evaluation is a strong indication that theological education by extension will continue to be a movement for change.

The Challenge

In recent years churches of many different traditions have established hundreds of new extension/distance/open/diversified programs in order to provide formation and training for pastors and other leaders for ministries in widely varied and often multicultural contexts. These programs have faced opportunities and obstacles that more traditional, centralized programs have not had to deal with. These challenges have, in fact, opened up new perspectives on the nature, possibilities, priorities, and issues of ministerial formation. Church leaders and theological educators have long felt the need for an evaluation of their extension programs, but the criteria and perspectives normally utilized for the evaluation and accreditation of theological institutions seem to be inadequate or even in some cases counter-productive. The consultation in Costa Rica provided an opportunity to gather reports and evaluations of theological education by extension programs in different parts of the world, examine issues that have arisen, and recommend models, instruments, and procedures for future evaluations.

From its inception the TEE movement has been motivated by the urgent need to make theological education, leadership, and recognized ministry accessible to all churches and all sectors of the churches— not just to a select few who become professional pastors. The Theological Community of Chile, after 15 years of TEE, reports a current enrollment of 4400 students, largely Pentecostal leaders who live and work among the poor. The Ghana Association of TEE indicates that that West African country has 15 residential theological schools, but they are not adequate for the task of evangelization and leadership training for Ghana's 22000 villages. The Organization of African Instituted Churches initiated its TEE project ten years ago because traditional theological education was found to be ineffective or counterproductive for these 8000 new denominations with a total constituency of 40 million people. In the U.K. the Church of England now offers 15 residential and 15 extension programs, some of the latter for lay training and others for ordinands or potential clergy. India's Board of Theological Education coordinates and acredits the work of some 35 formal, degree-oriented theological institutions; 15 of these have extension programs; and there is a constant challenge to create new programs to meet the vast needs of that sub-continent, whose population now approaches one billion. Pacific Theological College on the island of Fiji, the dean of theological institutions in the Pacific, reports that it is developing TEE to serve those islands, scattered over thousands of kilometers, that have no theological school. In the U.S.A. the Nazarene Bible College has developed a multicultural extension program with centers in 17 locations from New York to Hawaii and Detroit to Miami; 75% of its 630 students represent 16 non-Anglo population groups; classes are taught in five languages.

Basic Issues

After hearing reports from these and many other extension programs around the world, the consultation participants gathered perspectives, goals, and criteria for evaluation out of attempts that have already been made. They focused not primarily on numbers of people reached but rather on the nature and quality of these programs in relation to their contexts and constituencies. Several basic issues emerged, each with its own dynamics and tensions.

1. There was general agreement that evaluation should be based in the community being served with respect to the definition of goals and the assessment of results. Theological education programs should grow out of and respond to the needs of the Christian community and the larger human community, so the evaluation process must involve not only teachers and students but also the churches and their social contexts. This process should engage the different sectors of the community in dialogue about the programs from their different perspectives. This dialogue will normally include the tension between responsive accompaniment and prophetic challenge.

2. One of the most fundamental issues is the degree to which theological education programs fulfill their purpose with respect to God's mission in human history and with respect to the mission of the church. The overriding assumption is that these programs are preparing people to carry out God's purposes for humankind and for the church within that larger framework. Evaluation thus faces the tension between serving church and society as they are and as they ought to be.

3. Another basic and complex issue is the relation, consistency, or congruence between the theological and missiological foundations of a program and its practice. It is essential for evaluators to trace these foundations from institutional vision and goals through structures and program goals, curriculum and budget, selection of teachers and admission of students, educational processes and materials, to long and short term general and specific outcomes. The program should obviously model or exemplify the message and ministry it is trying to develop. Programs and people will always exhibit gaps between the ideals they affirm and the way they act; evaluation should help to narrow the gaps.

4. The development of alternative, decentralized forms of theological education has helped to identify and respond to the tendency of churches and theological institutions, like other human structures, to create and defend the interests of some at the expense of others. In modern societies the power and privileges of the professions are protected by academic institutions inaccessable to the majority. One of the major concerns of TEE has been to open the doors of theological education, leadership, and recognized ministry to those we have been excluded by social, economic, geographic, cultural, educational, gender, and other factors. Evaluation of TEE must ask whether these limitations are being overcome and also whether other interest are being created and defended by the new styles and structures of theological education.

5. Finally, the participants at the consultation recommended that TEE programs be evaluated in terms of both contextualization and globalization. It has been affirmed repeatedly that doing theological education in the context of local struggles, socio-cultural realities, and the practice of ministry can be very beneficial; this must be evaluated. On the other hand theological education must break the bonds of parroquialism and deal with global realities, the larger issues of our time, and the world church; this too must be evaluated in TEE.

Who? What? How?

Evaluation should go hand in hand with planning; it should be a basic component of the entire educational process. When students work on action and reflection or reading and research projects, when teachers and students discuss course material and issues in any academic area, when faculties and administrators and student bodies reflect on their work, when institutional boards and church bodies make decisions about these programs, when graduates consider their own effectiveness in ministry and when they are observed by their congregations and colleagues, evaluation takes place. Throughout the consultation many different aspects of TEE were identified for evaluation, with the assumption that greater improvement is possible through more careful, systematic evaluation.

1. Who should evaluate? In community-based evaluation all those who are affected by the program should participate in the process of evaluation. Three important, concentric circles of evaluators of TEE programs can be identified: first the churches and communities served, second the students and graduates, and third the teaching and administrative staff and governing bodies or committees of the program. The inclusion of at least selective participants from all three circles will not only assure essential input from these varied perspectives but also increase support and commitment for the program in general and for changes that emerge from the evaluation in particular. In addition outside persons can be invited to add special expertise and independent perspectives to the evaluation process.

2. What should be evaluated? The consultation did not attempt to draw up a complete list of things to be evaluated, though many aspects of TEE were mentioned. One comprehensive evaluation project presented at the consultation carried out extensive research on text materials and teaching methodology. Another evaluation proposal plans to gather data on the factors causing extension students to fall back or drop out. A more general evaluation plan asks different sectors of the community to answer these basic questions, each one with an appropriate questionnaire, then calls for a comparison between these expectations, current plans, and outcomes.

   • What should be the primary goal of the TEE program?
   • Who should the students be?
   • What should be taught?
   • How should the program's academic content, practical skills, and concern for spiritual formation be presented and what is the best educational process?
   • How should center leaders/teachers be selected and what characteristics should they possess?
   • What kinds of text materials should be used?
   • How should the TEE program be related to the local churches and to the local community?
   • Who should participate in planning and decision making?
   • What impact should the program have on students, churches, and the surrounding community?

3. How should evaluation be done? On the one hand the consultation participants were convinced that more comprehensive and systematic evaluation processes are needed. On the other hand they noted that the cost in time, emergy, or money must not go beyond the realistic expectations of any program to be evaluated. Therefore they recommended that simple and inexpensive as well as complex and more expensive models be made available. Both the simple and complex models should go beyond general descriptions to testing and analysis of specific aspects of the program.

Recommendations

The participants at the San José consultation recognized that this was but one stage in an ongoing process of maturation in TEE programs. In order to extend this process, the participants recommended the following.

1. A handbook on evaluation for use by TEE programs should be prepared. It should contain some theoretical foundations but concentrate largely on tools and methods that can be easily used by theological institutions to evaluate different aspects of their programs.

2. A book on TEE evaluation, incorporating some of the papers and group work of this consultation, should be published for use by theological educators and church leaders.

3. To promote development of TEE personnel, south-south visits between TEE programs across Asia-Africa-Latin America for the purpose of acquiring and sharing insights and experiences of one area with those of another area should be encouraged.

4. Women's, minorities' and marginalized groups' participation in each TEE program should be evaluated carefully with regard to admissions policies, program design and content, language, materials, methods, schedules, etc.